CURVES ON THE HIGHWAYS

A Self-Help Guide for Female Automobile Travelers

Gerry Hempel Davis

Drawings by Anna-Maria L. Crum

ROBERTS RINEHART PUBLISHERS

Published by Roberts Rinehart Publishers
An imprint of the Rowman & Littlefield Publishing Group
4720 Boston Way
Lanham, MD 20706

Distributed by National Book Network

Library of Congress Control Number: 2001097800

ISBN 1-57098-406-9 (pbk. : alk. paper)

∞™ The paper used in this publication meets the minimum requirements of
American National Standard for Information Sciences—Permanence of
Paper for Printed Library Materials, ANSI/NISO Z39.48-1992.
Manufactured in the United States of America.

Contents

Introduction   vii

One
Trip Planning   1

Two
On the Road   39

Three
Female Friendly Finds   53

DEDICATED TO
CLINT, MARK, MICHELLE

What would I do without you? You give me courage, inspiration, laughs, challenges, and applause. Most of all you are each true treasures in my life.

Master Alexander: There are no words to describe your wonderfulness and what you give, share, and teach this grandmother. A cherished treasure. May you always be safe and healthy.

*

THANK YOU TO
Rick Rinehart: Publisher, Editor extraordinaire. He realizes a good idea, gives you the go ahead and then helps and guides you to get the thoughts and words that you have in your mind and soul on paper . . . and he always takes your phone calls.

So many people helped me. To list them all would be a book in itself. I hope each of you know how much I appreciate all your help enthusiasm, and support. Don't hesitate to ask my help.

Nancy Peck, Stacy Lippin, Nancy Rath: Three Curves who ventured with me on several highways of all variety. What drives!

*

Introduction

THE URGE WITHIN

If you are thinking seriously about the possibility of traveling alone by car, this book is for you. It is not for the traveling businesswoman who lives under the protective umbrella of her employer. It is for the hesitant, inexperienced woman traveler who is (nevertheless) driven by the urge to seek out the world by herself, or with another woman.

We all need time to ourselves—to explore our true self as well as what is around us. Those who say that they won't or can't find time to be alone probably need it more than they realize. Taking a trip by yourself only requires the desire, some reasonable preparation, and careful execution. Money is of course required, but probably not as much as you think.

If you get approximately 400 miles to a tank of gas, you will need about 7 tanks of gas to get across the US. Depending on how direct your route is, an 18-gallon tank at $2.00 / gallon = $36.00 X 7 = $252.00 to make the journey.

So if you have the dreams, desire, determination and the dollars and just need to deal with the anxiety of traveling solo, or just being a female and traveling, accept the wisdom of the late Ella Fitzgerald: "It isn't where you come from, it is where you are going that counts."

Ask yourself: "What am I afraid of? Why am I fearful?" Are you afraid you are going to have an accident? Something is going to happen? You are going to get lost? Whatever you are afraid of happening while you are traveling can probably happen right at home.

Consider how many things you do by yourself that do not cause you any anxiety: you drive alone to work, to the grocery store, to a friend's place or to shopping. An odyssey of 500, 1000, or 3000 miles alone then should not be a problem. Indeed, there are many advantages to traveling alone, chief among them the fact that no one can tell you what to do, where to go, or when to eat and sleep.

Of course, we all have obligations and commitments that further contribute to our anxiety about doing anything so self-indulgent as taking an interesting road trip by ourselves or with another female. In life the "want-tos" tend to be subordinated to the "have-tos," but if you can stop accumulating the have-tos, there will be more room for the want-tos. The least desirable state is the "I wish I hads." You want to accumulate the "I'm glad I dids."

Traveling by yourself doesn't necessarily mean you'll be alone all the time. As you venture out, you are going to discover many other females out there and yes, many are alone. At the movies. In a restaurant. Driving on the highways. You haven't previously noticed because you weren't looking, but you will be surprised how many women you will see on the highways, driving by themselves.

Being alone does not mean being lonely. Nor is it necessarily antisocial or reclusive behavior. It can mean that you are just becoming more selective in sharing yourself with others.

My first real trip by myself proved to be wonderful, rewarding and therapeutic. It occurred the year my husband of 25+ years had decided to change his address, a few months after the marriage was officially dissolved. All was set in stone, except my self-esteem. I felt I had let everybody down. Thank goodness for the support of my parents and my sons.

There was no question about it. I had to go and check a rental property that I had acquired in the divorce. The property was not around the corner but a thousand miles away. My boys were in school. Thank goodness my mother could stay with them. I remember writing a zillion notes, kissing everyone goodbye a little after dawn and getting in the big old Mercury station wagon and starting down the highway. I had traveled the same route with my boys, but never by myself. Chills, flashes of whatever ran through me. Within thirty minutes, as the sun came up, I was going through a drive-thru getting coffee and a breakfast meal. In twenty minutes I was on the Interstate. Sometime during the next hour, a new feeling started to creep around and then permeate my body. I felt myself being healed, invigorated, rejuvenated – call it whatever you want, but a new me was developing. Perhaps it was the real me.

A little before midnight I was at my destination. I had driven almost 1000 miles. (I do not recommend driving this distance in one day, but this time the mind, body and energy levels were all correct.) Mothers do not care what time their children call to let them know they are safe and sound. I did just that. Mother understood her daughter exactly and said, "call us tomorrow after you check everything. We love you."

During my very therapeutic drive, I not only discovered "me" (or at least what I thought might be me), I discovered that although I was alone I was *not lonely.*

There are advantages to traveling alone that do not immediately come to mind. Try a new hairstyle. Put on some funky nail polish. Improve your eating habits. Expand your outlook. Better your mindset. Take necessity stops "as needed," not just when the car needs gas. Eat where, when and what you want. No one is going to criticize you if you fold the map the wrong way.

Although I had been serenaded by the 3 C's Classical, Country and Church music, after that first trip I discovered the best sound while driving in the car can be no sound at all and, being alone, you have no one to argue with over the radio or CD player. I have traveled thousands of miles and never turned on a thing, except the ignition and my thoughts. Noise hinders and distracts. Noise is for noisy, frenetic, frenzied places. Noise hides and camouflages. This is a clearing time. Your car can be a great "think tank." You can purge your mind and soul of anything or anyone that pulls you down.

Middle-aged research subjects were put into dark sound-proof rooms for as long as two days and nights. When they emerged they discovered sharper memories, improved

creativity and enhanced understanding of their relationships.
University of British Columbia, Vancouver

YOU'VE GOT TO CONTINUE TO GROW, OR YOU'RE JUST LIKE LAST NIGHT'S CORNBREAD - STALE AND DRY.

—*Loretta Lynn*

After having done the thousand-mile trek to my rental property a number of times, I started to wonder if I had it in me to take a solo trip across the U.S. and back. I certainly had the desire. I asked my world-traveled brother what he thought, and he simply, but poignantly stated, "It is just a drive." [R. C. Hempel]

It is, indeed, "just a drive."

One

TRIP PLANNING

So now your decision is made. You are going to take your trip. And of course you want it to be smooth and enjoyable, so preparation is very important. Planning a trip takes time and concentration and thought, but it is definitely serious fun.

Make this your motto: The Better You Plan, the Better the Trip.

Realize and acknowledge how much time you truly need to plan this odyssey. It is prudent, important and imperative to familiarize yourself with every aspect of your trip. You should ask for information and input from family members, friends, and travel agents, but planning your own trip is the very best way to make sure everything is the way you want and that all goes smoothly. It is only natural to briefly think about the why you are doing it and whether or not it will be all right.

Though driving is on the surface a sedentary pastime, long hours in the car can be strenuous. As soon as a trip is contemplated it is important to start "travel training," which means getting yourself into a regular routine of diet, exercise, and sleep.

It is also important to not discuss your upcoming trip with just anyone. Obviously, close friends and relatives will need to know, but making your plans any more public than that can be dangerous to your life and property. Picture this: you are standing in the checkout line at the grocery store. Enthusiastically you are telling a friend about your trip, unaware of who else may be listening. You pay your bill with a check. There in bold type is your address, glaring for all to see. Get the picture?

"I'm leaving tomorrow morning. It's going to be a great trip."

Notebooks: Key to Good Planning

One of the first things to do after deciding to travel is to buy two spiral notebooks. You know, the kind you used in school. There is simply no way any human being can possibly remember all of the details that are involved in planning a trip.

So keep one with you at all times to jot down: must do's, don't dos, thoughts, would likes, dislikes, don't forgets, and all sorts of information about the million and one things you have to keep track of. Keeping thoughts and everything straight is a task, but having a notebook will help you concentrate on the important things, not just where you left this or that important list or note.

Just as important is that after your trip these jottings will evoke memories. Believe it or not, you'll look back happily on these days of preparation and anticipation, and your jottings can be the preface to your trip diary and a jump-start for your next trip.

What about the second notebook? That's for your actual trip diary. This spiral diary can be put into a three-ring notebook that has pages with "pockets" for your travel memorabilia. (More on that later).

It is a must that you keep a diary of your trip. Although you think you'll remember each event, which is so vivid in your mind now, by the time you get home specifics blur and after you have taken a trip two and three, you'll be very grateful for the notes and pictures in your trip diary.

Make or photocopy a calendar showing the days you are to be away and where you plan to be. This is a handy item to have. Leave it with family and friends. I try to include as many confirmed places with phone numbers as possible. It is so much fun to get a call from a friend while you are on the road or in your room at night. My sons call me and sometimes when I check in somewhere there is a message from one of them: "Hi Mom. Just checking."

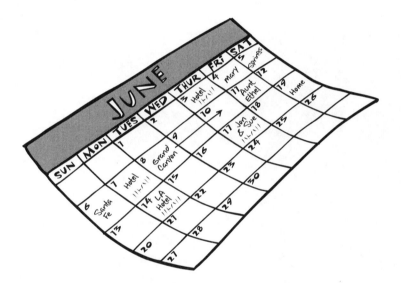

THINGS TO DO FIRST

1. Put your car keys on an elastic cord. Be sure keys are secure and cannot come loose. Get in the habit of putting your keys around your neck, except, of course, when your car keys are in the ignition, or you are in the bath, having a massage, etc. Don't put them in your pocket. Don't throw them in a bag. Don't hang them on a hook. WEAR THEM.

If you have ever lost or misplaced your car keys (or any important keys) you know that having them replaced (and perhaps even changing locks) is a big headache. Securing your keys in this manner will also allow you to leave your hands free.

Take only the necessary keys. You do not need your garage key, office key, desk key, etc. For security reasons, do not put

your name and address on your key chain. It's alright to have a phone number of your office or a friend, but you don't want to give any clues about what that anonymous set of keys is for.

Take an extra set of keys. Put it in a safe, handy spot that you can get at easily but that isn't obvious. If you have a coded key, know your key code. Put a copy of code in your pocketbook. This makes replacement easy.

Leave a set of keys at home with someone you will be able to reach in an emergency. If you lose both sets of keys, then you'll be able to have this set overnighted to you right away. This is certainly better and cheaper than paying a locksmith to get into your car and having a new key made.

If you have a numerical keypad on your car door, like I do on my Taurus, you should keep a copy of the original number in your bag. We all have an occasional blank brain moment.

2. Join AAA (American Automobile Association). Owning a car makes it a must to join AAA. Are you a member? If not, be sure you are a member before noon tomorrow! Be sure to obtain the "Plus Program." The Plus Program covers your car if it breaks down, *anywhere*. With the Plus Program, there will be no cost for the AAA "wrecker" to come to your aid. (Also check if your car has a Roadside Assistance Plan. My Taurus does and it is comforting to know I can dial 1-800-241-FORD and get help.)

The inconvenience and cost of a breakdown far from help (cars seldom break down in front of open gas stations, such as they are nowadays) is well worth a modest "insurance policy" to guarantee roadside assistance. Your AAA investment will be approximately $50.00. Visiting an AAA office you will learn about the benefits and options that this super organization provides. There are lots of perks and information to be had from hotel/motel accommodations to amusement attractions. AAA also has free books on each state that include specific information, attractions, lodging, etc. Later when you know exactly where you will be going you can get a great deal of specific information from these books. AAA offers many other benefits to car owners, such as insurance, credit cards, car buying, assistance, and free travelers checks.

Once you join AAA, you will receive a membership card and a sticker for your bumper. Put the card in your wallet and your sticker on your car's back bumper. If you do need roadside assistance, AAA will look for the sticker and ask for your card.

3. Purchase a large road atlas. The AAA atlas (as of this writing) has changed its size and is now on the small side. I suggest that you purchase a large atlas, easily found at Barnes & Noble or one of the other book chains or shopping clubs. It has a lot of additional information and is definitely easier to read.

From AAA obtain a single large USA map (free to members). You should also obtain individual large state maps, also free to AAA members. These will be extremely helpful as they show the smaller towns and roadways in detail.

Make 5 to 8 photocopies of the large USA map in the front of your atlas. This map is a more practical size to use in the planning than the very large AAA USA map and better than a small map. Mark the following on one map or on individual maps—whichever is best for you. Eventually you will combine on one or two maps. A.) Mark in one color where you have already been; b.) Mark in another color where you would like to go; c.) Mark in another color where you have friends or friends of friends that you might like to visit; and d.) More important, highlight friends that would truly like for you to visit. Note: When you mark your maps DO NOT use a broad felt pen, as it will obliterate important map markings. This is very important for your final map. Your final travel map can be all the above combined.

I was going out west to do research for a book and to attend a wedding in Jackson Hole, Wyoming. While I was looking at the maps and planning my routes, I realized that Boise, Idaho was not really that far out of the way. It would be a 6-8 hour drive but I would see one of my favorite classmates. When I called her; her enthusiasm left no doubt in my mind, that "Boise here I come." What a visit! I took class pictures that I had and to say we had fun is an understatement. The following summer; just before I was to leave on another westward trip, my Boise Classmate called. She was in the hospital. Her end came faster than was expected. The detour to Boise is one I will be forever grateful to have taken.

AAA publishes maps of every state in the country, and lots of detailed maps of cities and regions too. They will prepare for you, if you ask them, something called a Triptik, which is a customized grouping of maps showing your planned route. Don't ask me why, but I do not use these Triptiks. Perhaps I feel I become more familiar with my specific trip if I plan it myself; I also think Triptiks are hard to follow on the road. This is just my feeling, though. Many people swear by Triptiks.

AAA also publishes travel guides that describe attractions and cities, and have listings and ratings of hotels and restaurants just about everywhere. These are just as good as most of the travel books you'll find in the bookstore, and best of all they're paid for in your membership. In addition, they have 1100 offices all over the country, so if you need help during your trip, chances are you'll find AAA nearby.

Begin to familiarize yourself with map reading. Know what each line and color represents. Learn to read a map correctly and quickly. This only comes with practice. Begin practicing NOW. You cannot practice too much.

4. Start budgeting your trip. An essential part of travel planning is budgeting of both time and money. TIME: From the time you turn the ignition on in your car till the time you walk back through your front door, calculate the time. MONEY: How much money do you *really* have to spend on this trip? Accuracy is the key here. You must know how much you can afford to spend on the trip, but you must also budget for the unexpected (both good and bad) because something will happen that you didn't plan for: a breakdown, a forgotten bill, or even that great "find" at a shop you'll probably never visit again. So be sure to make as accurate a budget as possible. Include estimates for the following categories:

Gas: ($1.75 per gallon)
Other car maintenance (oil, wiper blades, etc.): no less than $300
Food: $50.00 average per day. More for a few special dining outs.
Lodging: $100 per day (on the high side, but you never know).
Souvenirs: It is your money, but $300 would be on the safe side if you don't get carried away with trinkets.

Film and film developing: $2.50 per roll of film. $10.00 per roll developing.

Admission fees to attractions: Call ahead or check web sites and guide books.

Other trip-related cost considerations include a home alarm system, travel clothes, pre-trip car servicing, AAA membership, travel sundries, and plastic packing boxes (see packing chapter), cell phone, cameras, etc.

5. Obtain a cell phone. The type of route you take to your destination will determine the type of phone you take. There are two basic types: analog and digital. Analog cell phone service is more widespread, but digital is cheaper on a per minute basis and has better sound and features. New dual band phones offer both systems. I would go into more detail but advances in equipment and service are made so quickly what I tell you now will probably be out of date tomorrow. Since competition is stiff in this business, for the best deal be sure to check out at least two reputable cell phone dealers. (In many places, AAA offers a good deal on their own cell phone services.)

During my long research driving trips, I take two phones. One is the best cell phone available. The other is the best heavy-duty model that has more range. For the few dollars extra that it costs to take two, the security it gives me is worth the expense.

After obtaining your cell phone, make yourself familiar with its features. Know how to call the police quickly. Make a habit of automatically charging it whenever you stop for the night. Buy a cigarette lighter adapter as well, which will recharge your phone as well as provide a back-up power source if your cell phone battery fails.

In your car, keep an emergency instruction card by the phone. [See Clue Card] It's natural to forget sometimes, so if you are in a twit or a panic, an instruction card will remind you how to use it. The phone "clue card" should be taped by the phone or on the dashboard. Do not place it in the glove compartment: it might get lost among the clutter. (see "clue cards" pages.)

I was recently in Nashville and saw the man in the car next to me, in a disgusted gesture, throw down his cell phone. Then I saw the flashing red lights of the police car behind him.

Also be aware that some cities and states do not allow driving and phoning at the same time. Fortunately, many companies like the Ford Motor Company are developing handsfree adaptors with their cars. I prefer these adaptors because they are integrated into the car's audio system and thus provide the best sound. When a call comes in, it even mutes the stereo for you. In any case, it's never a good idea to "drive and phone." It just isn't safe. You are on new highways and in new places. Keep your mind on the road. If you get a call, get in the right lane and, if possible, onto the shoulder or frontage road before answering. You might have to answer and say "please wait" and then get over to continue the conversation. If you get disconnected don't worry. If it's an important call, you'll get a call back, and most phones have caller ID so you won't have to write down the number of whoever called you.

PLANNING THE ROUTE: STARTS, STOPS, STARTS, STOPS, AND RETURN

On a piece of paper make a list of the places you want to visit in order of priority. (Or use one of your photocopied maps.) Be sure to have your travel notebook handy to jot down thoughts as you plan your route.

> TO DRINK IN THE SPIRIT OF A PLACE YOU SHOULD NOT ONLY BE ALONE BUT NOT HURRIED.
> —*George Santayana*

Here's the fun part: spread the maps out on the floor or a large table. Look at each map carefully. Take your time. When I plan a trip, my maps become permanent exhibits on my floor or on a large table. As you look at each map, your itinerary will start to take shape. You'll start to see what's feasible and what isn't, what is efficient and what will waste your time.

Distance and driving times can be calculated from the maps, from the mileage chart at the front of the atlas, or from a Rand McNally DIST-O-MAP which costs about $7.95.

The highways in the United States are (for the most part) of sound construction and well marked. You can see on the maps what a comprehensive highway system this country has designed.

Consult the AAA personnel for road updates. Construction sites can cause delays, but don't let it annoy you—just think of it as the price you pay for such a fine road system.

IMPORTANT: Some designated scenic highways (in road atlases) are not necessarily what I would call sensible *easy* roads. There are roads I call *brake burners*. These roads are full of twists and curves. *White knuckle* roads are even worse. They not only have twists and curves, but low guardrails and narrow pullover spots. My Taurus has a 200 horsepower engine that makes climbing hills a breeze. On these roads, be sure to downshift to a lower gear to take advantage of a phenomenon known as "engine braking," which will help save your brakes. If you're reluctant to drive on these roads, make sure you've obtained good information about all of the roads you'll be using. It can be terrifying to get onto a dangerous road with no way out except to go forward.

After you've obtained the information you need about distances and roads, you will be able to set a schedule for yourself. At this point it's only tentative: lots can change before you get on the road, but this is a good start.

With your list and map in hand now you start your actual scheduling. When calculating stops, remember that you can usually average 65- 70 miles per hour for travel on interstate highways.

Begin:
　　How many days will you be gone?_____

Prepare a schedule for *every* day.

DAY 1: Departure time_____
　　　　Miles To Major Stop # 1_____
　　　　Sightseeing at:_____ Time Allotted_____

　　　　Miles To Major Stop #2:_____
　　　　Sightseeing at:_____
　　　　Spending night at:_____

DAY 2: Leave_____
　　　　Miles To_____
　　　　etc.

In your schedule, try to include approximate times for gas, rest breaks, lunch, etc. I figure a stop of 15 minutes for gas every 300 miles; a drive-through lunch of 15 minutes; a restaurant meal of 30+ minutes; bathroom break of 15 minutes, etc. Estimated times of arrival and departure will keep you on track. If possible try to budget an extra hour or two as your "free" time per day or perhaps every other day. Sometimes you will use it, sometimes you won't. But it is nice to have. The more you travel the more you will be able to pace your day. You want to see as much as possible on this trip and not get exhausted. The way to do it is to keep to your schedule. Don't try to cram in too much. But also don't shortchange yourself. Remember what Thomas Jefferson said: "Determine never to be idle . . . it is wonderful how much may be done if we are always doing."

The flip side of scheduling is flexibility, which is just as important. If a detour of any sort needs to be made, don't get annoyed and bent out of shape. Something wonderful and better might serendipitously take place.

Now that you have determined your route, you're ready to get down to brass tacks: besides driving, what are you going to do, and where will you stay? You will need to gather lots of information—the more the better—about the places you'll be visiting. Remember: *you can never have too much information!* Here are some tips about obtaining information and what to obtain.

Find out about attractions and special sights to see that are on your route from AAA brochures and books, other guidebooks, the internet, or friends. Call for particulars such as days and hours of operation, admission fees, weather, distance from interstates, and whether tours are available. I also find it important to always ask for specific directions, particularly if a sight is well off the beaten path.

Your travel time is valuable. You don't want to have to wait a long time for a tour to begin, or worse, find that the attraction is closed. Major attractions usually have a toll-free telephone number. Check with the local Chamber Of Commerce. Call and get information on festivals and other special events in the area during your visit. Carry every phone number you have used in planning your trip. Write them down as you use them and add notes.

Planning for Where You Will Be Staying: Choosing the Right Place To Stay

Your choice of lodging will depend on a lot of factors: price, location, amenities, etc. It seems risky to plan to stay at a place you've never even seen: there are a lot of crummy hotels out there, and you don't want to end up in one of them. Staying at established hotels or motels or chains is the best way to ensure that you won't. It's not foolproof, but it usually works.

Where will you be staying? Research. Check with friends, AAA, etc. Most hotels and motels have toll-free numbers for reservations. If by any slim chance there is not a toll free number for a place you hope to visit, spend the pennies and call and obtain information. Call to be certain you can get accommodations. When you first call a hotel, you are usually quoted the "rack rate", which is the highest rate they have, so don't hesitate to ask about any special deals that might be available. Don't forget to use any AAA or AARP discounts, or coupons that you have or that you might have picked up along the way.

A good book to have is published by Entertainment Publications (see entertainment.com). They publish guides to over a hundred metropolitan U.S. areas, and each one contains a zillion coupons for restaurants and other local attractions, and for national chains. More important for you, though, are the hotel listings: they have about 5000 hotels that will give you a 50% discount just for showing the "entertainment" membership card that comes in every book. Of course each hotel has some restrictions on dates, but you'll save the $29.95 cost of the book if you use it just once!

When you know your plans, it's a good idea to make reservations. Don't forget to get a firm price and a confirmation number. A confirmation fax or e-mail is also good to have and to put in your travel book. Do not be shy about getting names of those you speak with when you make reservations.

Remember to keep all phone numbers in the notebook or electronic organizer that you use to plan your trip as well as any other numbers that you discover might be of help, including your friends' numbers along the way. (Wouldn't you hate to find they have an unlisted number!) Take important names and phone numbers of doctor, dentist etc. and friends at home, just in case you have to call home. In addition, You might pre-program these names into your cellular phone. It may be a little paranoid, but I would not hesitate (and I don't!) to make a copy of this and put the extra copy under the seat or someplace in the car . . . just in case. Phone books are usually missing in phone booths and directory information costs too much to call. Your personal phonebook is also essential. Make a photocopy of your book and take the copied version with you. (I once lost my personal phone book, and I can tell you it's an awful thing to have happen.) I often put my hometown phone directory in the car as well. Of course you can always use it as a booster seat.

By now you should be feeling comfortable with the fact that a road adventure is not only feasible, but just might be essential to your personal well-being. Do not expect that the planning of your odyssey will be accomplished quickly. If you want to have an efficient, productive, fun and hopefully very safe trip, then thorough and sometimes tedious planning is absolutely key.

It will not take you much longer to have your plan all in place. Any hesitations that you have will be soothed because questions will be answered and plans will be in place. More important is that the unknown does not seem so frightening. Soon the *unknown* will be the *known!*

Planning for Packing
There is an old adage among experienced travelers: always take more money and fewer clothes than you think you will need. The following section, while not denying you your favorite items, will at least tell you how to pack them sensibly and economically.

1. Collect plastic containers and bottles of all sizes. Small containers and bottles are useful for quick overnight stays and short trips, where small amounts of the items that you use daily—shampoo, conditioner, mouth wash, lotions, etc.—can be "downloaded" from the larger, store-bought bottles. A small bottle for clothes powders or liquid soap and fabric softener is handy if you want to wash a pair of undies.

For longer trips you will have the large product bottles in your Supply Box (of this, more later). You will replenish small bottles as needed. Remember: mark all bottles and baggies clearly.

During one trip I had several bad hair days, and I'm one whose hair can set the mood! I wash my hair daily and condition when needed. By not marking my shampoo and conditioner bottles I "washed" my hair with the conditioner. At first I attributed the limp, lumpy hair to the water and weather. If I had just put on S and C on the bottles.

Other useful hints:

—A spice jar that has a sprinkle-top makes a wonderful powder jar.

—You can take the smallest of bottles filled with mouth-wash for your pocketbook to refresh during the day.

—For water use small plastic Coke bottles or refill empty water bottles. If you are where you can freeze plastic bottles of water, be sure to do so. (Remember to not completely fill a bottle of water that is to be frozen.)

—Small spray-pump plastic bottles are useful to mist your face with water in hot climates. However, pump bottles tend to mysteriously discharge their contents while in your suitcase or pocketbook, so be sure store them in a zip-lock bag.

—Empty film containers are an ideal size for safety pins or pills.

—Keep a stash of instant coffee in a small bottle or jar.

—Lip Balm. Use generously. When traveling, lips become parched that never did so before.

—Cream: For face, hands, ankles, etc.

3. Save the plastic sleeves your newspapers arrive in. These are very useful for packing shoes, stockings, hair bows, curlers etc. Ditto plastic grocery bags, which are better for clunky hiking or exercise shoes that tend to be more aromatic than the rest of your clothing. (They also make convenient, automobile-sized trash bags.) Zip-lock bags of all sizes and shapes are also essential.

4. For long trips, use large clear plastic boxes as "travel closets." A 24 X 14 box costs about $5. I tend to use several of these on a trip and organize them thusly: daytime and night time clothing; outerwear; underwear and scarves; shoes and bags. When I arrive at my destination it's a fairly simple matter to transfer what I need into a small overnight bag. Of course, the size and number of boxes you use will depend on the space available in your car (I drive the Ford Taurus station wagon pictured on the front cover, so I have quite a bit of room).

Do you remember that line in "The Graduate" where a man comes up to young Ben and says: "I have just one word to say to you young man: plastics." Well, that's how I feel about packing: the key is to have lots of clear plastic boxes in the right sizes. I use them both for pre-trip organizing and for actual packing.

Why plastic boxes? Plastic boxes are clean, economical, and practical. You will need a fair amount of clothing for your adventure, but you do not need everything every day. You do not want to lug a big bag of toiletries, a big bag full of clothes, etc. to your room every night. It's easy to see what is inside a plastic box and to pull out just what you need.

When you arrive at a destination you take out of the appropriate box only what you need, and put it in a small bag. If you find you need something else all you have to do is go and get it. If the weather changes or your mood has changed, or you suddenly have a special invitation, the right clothes are easily found. This method is especially handy if you are traveling for a considerable time and in different climates.

The exact box size you will need depends on where they must fit and what you are taking, but here are some guidelines:

a) Buy four or five large clear plastic storage boxes for clothing, about 24 inches long by 14 inches wide. I call these Gerry's Travel Closets. When you start to figure out what you're going to take on your adventure, place the clothing items that you *think* you are going to take in one of the boxes, which are each designated with a clothing category. Again categories I usually start with are: daytime

I confess I don't always practice what I preach. My first major long trip I took so much more than I needed. But I've learned from experience and hopefully am getting better. I envy those who can pack in a tea bag.

clothing, nighttime clothing, outerwear, underwear, shoes and bags.

There are lots of benefits to this system, even if you're not actually taking these boxes with you. First, you are organized from the very beginning, and are able to judge at a glance whether you're heavy on one type of clothes or another. Second, it's flexible. You can always add items and take them out, and even change the categories, as you better understand your needs. And of course it keeps everything from piling up all over the house, or having to repack one huge suitcase.

b) Medium clear plastic storage boxes are useful for other items. Standard 16 X 11 boxes can be used for toiletries, prescription medicines, important papers, and what I refer to as a "just in case" box for such items as scissors, stamps, plastic utensils, etc. (See list below.)

Organize your boxes with titles such as: Essential, Crucial, (Toiletries) Supply Box, Buddy Box, Just in Case Box.

You also might have a "Pocketbook" Box for the items that you will keep with you all the time: travelers checks, pepper spray, regular checks, your notes, make-up, safety pins for pinning items in your bag, etc.

A small and a mid-size ice chest/thermal chest are indispensable.

An Essential Box and a Crucial Box are helpful, even if just in the preparation and planning. The Essentials are items that you should take but might be expensive and difficult to replace. The Crucial Box contains items that you must take because your life (or at the least, very good health) may depend on them. Your Crucial Box should contain things like prescription and over-the-counter medicines, vitamins, and so forth. (Be sure to keep copies of your prescriptions as well. If you have a Walgreen's prescription it can be filled at any of their stores in the U.S.) No matter how long or short the trip is, I prepare my individual vitamin packs in aluminum foil. In some cases it may be necessary to keep your medicines cool, and for this I recommend a small ice chest or thermal cooler. (On one of my trips I had left some vitamins in a navy blue plastic box, and after experiencing several 100-degree days found that all the gel caps had melted. Not pretty or terribly aromatic.)

There will be some items that you will continue to use prior to leaving that will eventually need to go into these boxes. If you don't actually put the item in the box now, write a note for each item. Only when you put the item in the box, do you remove the note.

You will have your small toiletries bag packed for your daily needs. You go to the Supply Box when something needs to be replenished. Be certain you have fully stocked toiletry supplies. Travel time is precious and shopping for toiletries is not on the itinerary.

Toiletries suggestions

Mouth Wash
Nail Scissors, Emory Boards & File
Shampoo
Moleskin (for the feet)
Conditioner
Safety Pins
Razors
Pepto-Bismol
Neosporin
Milk of Magnesia
Vaseline
Lotions
Band-Aids
Bug Spray
Calamine Lotion
Sun Screen
Individual baggies full of Epsom Salts (for soaking your feet or body)
Lip Balm
BFI
Tweezers
Wooden matches

BFI (Bismuth-Formic-Iodine) is great stuff but not so easy to find. Once, when I was in Northern Maine I had a blister and a cut. I went into a drug store and asked the pharmacist for BFI. "You're too young to know about BFI," he said. I told him that my mother had taught me about it, to which he replied: "I always have some on the shelf for knowledgeable people." I hope you can find some.

Hair color tip: if you use bottled hair color, it's better to take your regular product than to try to locate the same thing out on the road. (Speaking of "hair," if you've ever wanted to try a really new hairstyle, or some funky clothes, on your trip is the time to do it!)

Your Buddy Box sits next to you on the front seat or just behind you. It has all those little useful items and should be easily accessible. Suggestions for what to put in it include a heavy-duty flashlight, extra batteries (for everything, not just the flashlight), Handy Wipes, Kleenex, a small wash cloth in a Ziploc bag, plastic utensils, straws, an all purpose can or bottle opener, etc. And because the cleanliness and inclusiveness of bathrooms will vary tremendously on your journey, you may also want to put in a small bag such items as toilet paper, Vaseline, soap, hand lotion and other feminine items. Finally, too big for a box, but a two good items to have on hand: a roll of paper towels and an umbrella.

The Just in Case Box contains items that you might not need but if you do, they are worth their weight in gold. Included here are extra pair or pairs of glasses (regular and sunglasses), an eyeglass repair kit, scotch tape, pad of paper, some good stationery, permanent markers, pens, pencils, a sharp knife, heavy duty garbage bags (which can double as a makeshift poncho), rubber bands, envelopes, FedEx envelopes, bungee cords, gift wrap and ribbon (you never know...), and a full roll of duct tape.

In a hit and run accident my car door was scraped and the front bumper torn off. Miraculously I was not hurt. The door would lock if pushed hard, but the left front light was hanging by a wire. The State Trooper and I, though, were able to secure the loose light and some hanging chrome with duct tape. Don't leave home without it!

Other Ways to Pack
Remember: A bag that is heavy *before* you pack will only be worse packed.

Hard suitcase with rollers: A large suitcase is useful to hold all of your clothes. The problem is that you end up taking it with you each night, so I don't recommend using one. If you do take one, though, remember not to pack toiletries inside, and make sure all your baggage fits easily into your car.

Duffel Bags: Coming in all shapes and sizes, these are almost as useful as plastic bags. Be sure to take at least two extras along for new purchases you accumulate.

Hanging bag: Not my favorite. They don't hold very much and are awkward to carry. But if you use one, be sure it is sturdy and large and has a lot of pockets.

Closet rod: Don't hang clothes in the car. It shows and tells too much.

Thermal Cooler Chest: This is a must. Ideal for perishable travel foods or any items that might melt or sag in hot climates. Buy a light-colored one: dark colors attract and hold heat.

Cardboard boxes: If you are likely to purchase a lot, you might want to ship a box home. Consider taking a flattened cardboard box and packing tape. The flattened box takes up virtually no room and it's there if you need it.

Thermos Cups: At least two (one for cold one for hot) with tight-fitting lids that fit in the cup holder of your car!

ID Cards & Clue Cards

Make several ID cards using standard 3 X 5 note cards. Use indelible ink and cover with plastic clear tape, preferably the wide type of tape used to seal packages. A baggie can also be used but it is not quite as effective.

One card should contain nothing but such emergency information as doctor's name and number, name of a family contact and his or her number, special medical conditions and/or requirements (Allergies? Asthmatic? Diabetic?), health insurance company and group number, etc. This card should always be in your car. I keep one ID card sticking out of the glove compartment with the words EMERGENCY INFORMATION clearly visible. The only time you might consider taking this card with you is if you are going to have someone park your car.

This card will probably never be used, but neither will your spare tire. But you will have both, "just in case." Other sorts of documents that you should take along include insurance cards (both medical and auto) and perhaps even your passport. And double check that both your license and registration are up to date and easily accessible.

Emergency roadside signs are something you should have in your car at all times, not just for long trips. AAA has them, but you can also make your own with a long piece of cardboard or poster board cut in strips or left whole and some neon spray paint or large markers. "Call Police," "Emergency," or just plain "Help" are some possible suggestions.

I also make up what I refer to as "Clue Cards," that remind me of my cell phone features, emergency numbers, what to do, what certain key lock combinations are, etc. You never know what can happen to the brain after following that white line for 400 miles.

Pre-Packing

It's all coming together. You've decided where you're going and when, you've started to plan your route, and you've thought about where you might be staying. Now is the time to start collecting and organizing what you think you are going to take with you. It's time to start filling those plastic boxes.

There are two overarching rules to packing:

Rule #1: KISS (Keep it Simple and Sensible). Remember the adage "Always take more money and fewer clothes..." and make sure you have everything you will really need...but take no more than that. This is not always easy to accomplish, and I certainly don't always practice what I preach. If you're worried about under packing, just remember that you can probably purchase anything vital on the road. And if you're worried about over packing, good! You don't want to look like the camel trader who carries his entire inventory on his beast of burden. I feel like I've packed well if I return with very few items I haven't used, and that I haven't had to purchase too many things along the way.

Rule #2: Use up the items that have been cluttering your closet, dressers and medicine cabinet, and vow never to bring them back home! Whether we want to admit it or not, we all have items of clothing, from underwear to sweaters, that may be a little over used. Now is the time to pack them, use them one more time, and leave them. That is correct. Wear and throw out! Very therapeutic, and an excuse to buy new clothes as well!

I had a brainstorm just before I left on a long trip once. I went through the baskets of "items" that covered my bathroom vanity. Amazingly, I didn't find a thing growing. I put them all in a plastic bag and during the trip, whatever came out of the grab bag, I used. Most of the time you could hear me say, "why on earth did I get this?!"

Your Car, Your Companion

Your car will be your road-home, your soul mate for your trip. If you take good care of it, it will take good care of you. I can personally attest to this, having put 97,000 miles on my first Ford Taurus; I am now on my second. This is as true now, at the planning stage, as it will be on the road. So take the time to make sure everything is working properly.

Have your car completely checked out, either by your dealer or by a good mechanic. I personally prefer to have my Ford dealer do it because they have better training, equipment and knowledge of my car than anyone else. They can also get parts faster. Have them check *everything*. This is the time to fix whatever might need fixing, not when you're on the road and your time is very valuable. Road repairs can be expensive. And don't leave your car check-up until the last minute. Do it at least two weeks before you are supposed to leave. Why? Because a part might need to be ordered, or a procedure that requires some time to perform might be needed.

Educate yourself *now* about your car: know how to check all of the fluid levels (oil, coolant, windshield washer, transmission fluid) and how to add them if needed. Also learn to check your windshield wipers, headlights and taillights. If you're not quite sure how to perform any of these tasks, take your car to your local dealer and have them go over the car with you. My dealer is always happy to educate me about my car. In addition, I have the comfort of knowing there are about 4,600 other Ford dealers across the U.S. who can assist me if something happens. One is never far away!

Tires

Tires are a maintenance item unto themselves. You will need to check your car's manual to find out what the recommended tire pressure is and add (or subtract) air accordingly. Also, do the "tread check": take a penny and stick Lincoln's head in the tread. If you can read, above his hair, "In God We Trust" the treads are down and you need new tires. You should also know how a car "acts" when you have tire problems. This can start with a rhythmic noise or wobbling in the steering wheel. Finally, you should prepare yourself for buying tires in a strange town. Call up your car dealer or a reliable local tire dealer before you leave to get a price on replacement tires for

My recent repair story. Just before my last road odyssey, I took my car into the dealer to have it totally serviced even though it had been driving absolutely perfectly. Within hours of leaving my car, I was called and told that the serpeintine belt had cracks and should be replaced. Of course, it couldn't be something minor like a windshieldwiper or a headlight. But I was thrilled in spite of the cost: I knew what a disaster it would have been if the belt had broken while I was on the road.

I was once driving in northern Florida and stopped to get gas. I admit that the gas station looked a little shady. I was then a road novice. I had not established my rule of never letting the gas gauge get below 1/4 of a tank. Female ALONE! Alert! The gas attendant walked around my car; shaking his head. "Lady you have awful tires on your car: I hope you don't have to go very far. You might not make it." Before I knew it he had a tire book out, showing me the tires I should buy. Flustered a bit , I said I had to call my son.

"Mom, those tires will make it home, unless you run over nails. They are worn but okay. Drive carefully and all will be fine."

I quickly paid for the gas and off I went. And yes I did make it home. All was fine . . . But several lessons were learned.

1. Don't stop in suspicious gas stations.
2. Don't let the gas get below 1/4 of a tank.
3. Knowledge is power. Know your tires.

your vehicle. That way you'll know in advance what a reasonable price for a tire is. Don't forget to include the cost of tire balancing, valve stems, and installation. Get this information and put it in your car. You will not remember the facts under duress. Remember that the original tires specified for your vehicle will provide the best performance because they were "tuned" for your vehicle. Your selling dealer can give you a list of all the tires that were specified as original equipment on your car. Working on this book, I learned all sorts of things. Checking the "birth" date of tires is important; you do not want to buy tires that have been sitting around. If you check the last three digits on the sidewall serial number they will tell you the date of manufacture, calculated by week and year. For example: "168" means the tire was made the 16th week of 1998.

Windshield

A sudden dust storm or bug swarm will wreak havoc on your windshield. It's not safe to drive with a mucky windshield, so be sure to carry a good window cleaner for keeping windows clean inside and out. It also comes in handy for your glasses. Get in the habit of cleaning or at least checking your back and front windows and side mirrors every time you get gas. Also keep on hand a roll of paper towels. People say that the best cleaning "cloth" for windows is newspaper. The trouble is that you get ink all over your hands, so I stick with paper towels.

Jumper Cables

Jumper cables are a handy item to have. If you don't want to spend the $20 to buy some, perhaps you can borrow a set for your trip. There are handy all-in-one jump kits, but again you must know what you are doing. It's best to call your vehicle's roadside assistance number or AAA for car problems (but remember you have to be a member). But if your car has a dead battery due to a light being left on or something like that, and you have cables with you and are in a relatively safe place, someone can jump start your car. Usually if your car starts right up after it is "jumped" that usually means it was a temporary drain on the battery, and running the engine for at least 25 minutes will charge the battery again. You can drive during that time, but don't turn the car off for 25 minutes.

On one trip my air conditioner died. I was planning to get a new car "soon" and therefore did not want to spend the money on new A/C, which would have been a lot. I happened to be in Pep Boys looking for a boy-present for a friend's son and mentioned to the salesman about the A/C. A trucker was nearby and said: "Hey lady, why don't you get what the truckers have—a fan that's powered by the car's lighter." So that is just what I did. It did the job perfectly and saved me money as well.

Air Conditioner

Be sure to remind mechanics when your car is being serviced to completely check the A/C. You don't want this to fail you in the middle of Death Valley. A couple of air conditioning tips: get in the habit of turning your A/C off before turning the car off; starting your engine and the A/C at the same time puts a big strain on the battery and other components, though some may disagree with this. And don't keep your car so cold that you can almost see your breath. It may feel good while you are *in* the car, but when you get out the heat thwacks and envelops you and it is truly a shock to your system. Try low to medium cold.

Don't let the A/C blow on you point blank. (I believe this applies to any A/C.) The cold air blowing directly on you causes headaches, muscle aches, and body aches. Conversely, don't keep your car too warm; it induces drowsiness.

Other Car Concerns

1. Follow this sequence to starting your car: buckle your safety belt; turn on the ignition; turn on the headlights; make mirror adjustments; make seat adjustments; and, if applicable, adjust pedals. Also be certain all items are out of sight, nothing is hampering your view, and the front seat is not cluttered. Is your phone accessible? Are the items that you might need, i.e. maps, water, glasses, towel, near by?

2. Be aware of different driving laws in each of the states. While "right on red," for example, has become fairly universal, some states and cities still don't allow it or at least limit its application.

3. If your car requires servicing on a trip, your best bet is to go to the service department of a dealer of your type of car. Most mechanics are trustworthy, but going to a dealer's service department will provide you with an extra measure of assurance.

4. Listen to your car. Become accustomed to the way it sounds when running smoothly, so that when you hear an unfamiliar noise you will know something might be amiss.

5. Know how to check fluid levels. Your car's manual will tell you where to check levels and where to refill reservoirs (these may be two different places). This goes for oil and windshield washer fluid; transmission oil is best checked and refilled by a mechanic.

6. Be aware of your car's "blind spots." A car has yet to be built without blind spots, although most new cars now have "fish eye" parabolic mirrors on the right-hand side. These help a little, but the best thing is to drive with your head on a swivel. Mirrors alone don't tell you the whole story of what's coming up behind you.

Comfort in Your Car

How you sit is so important, whether at your desk or in your car. Here are a few sitting suggestions for long drives.

Seat

For the seat, I sit on two firm cushions that I put in a cotton pillowcase. The pillowcase keeps them from slipping apart and also cools. The height is just right, raising me to a better sitting and seeing position. My goal is to be like the truckers and sit high; it is easier to see and more comfortable.

Back

For the back of the driver's seat, my Taurus has an "orthopedic" adjustable lumbar support. I crank it up to the max and adjust the back to the straightest of positions, a straight right angle.

If you sit in a soft bucket seat with a cushy back, you will probably get seat and back fatigue very quickly. Soft may be fine for short drives, but not long drives. However, I have been told that bucket seats do provide more lateral support and keep you more firmly in place on winding roads. Sit straight, drive straight, and you'll feel straight.

Even if you choose not to use any of the "seat" suggestions, do consider using a cotton towel to cover the seat of your car. It is only natural that your seat gets warm and moist, especially if the car seats are velour. It is a double whammy if you are in 100 degrees heat. A towel for the passenger seat is also advisable. You'd be surprised at how much it "collects" and protects.

Finally, be sure the position of your steering wheel, relative to the position of your seat, allows for your arms to be relaxed and comfortably in control of the steering wheel. Not a straight stiff position. Many steering wheels are adjustable nowadays. A good rule of thumb to determine if you are in a good seating position is if your wrist can drape over the top of the wheel while your back is against the seat. The power adjustable pedals (what will they think of next!) on my new Taurus allows me to bring the pedals closer to me and I don't have to pull up the seat quite as much as I used to. I strongly feel that one should adjust the pedals only before putting the car in gear and not while driving. I'm told that a female Ford engineer developed this concept!

When you drive for long periods of time, you are liable to ache in places where you have never ached before. This is to be expected, but it doesn't have to last for long if you take care of it right away. The best thing is to take a break at least every two hours and walk around for ten minutes or so. Remind your body what it was like to walk and get the circulation moving. Your neck might require some work as well, so if you don't have an on-board masseuse roll it around a bit.

Planning for Safety and Security

There are a number of items that you should consider carrying for your own self-defense, but hopefully you'll never have to use them.

Pepper Spray

Essential for women traveling alone, whether to the grocery store or across the country. Obtain both a large canister and a small one. Keep the large one in your car between the seat and the console, wrapped in a scarf or washcloth. The small one should always be with you, either in your pocket or in "a quick to get to" part of your pocketbook. This handy item is essential for fending off people and animals. You might want to practice a bit so you don't end up pepper-spraying yourself.

Bells

Noise is a big deterrent to crime. You can create your own alarm system with bells. They come in all sizes, shapes and forms, and they can make a lot of noise unexpectedly. These are easy to find in a toy store or party store.

You can use a big cowbell or lots of small bells on a rope or a loose collection in an old stocking, tied at the end. This is easy to attach almost anywhere. Remember if you do carry bells with you, carry them in a confined manner. You do not want to walk into a place jingling.

I have a set of bells that at the slightest bump let off a lot of ringing. I have hung them on doors—just in case. You can even hang them inside your car door when you stop for a quick eye and body rest. (If you can sleep soundly in a rest stop and need bells to wake you up, you're lucky!)

Portable Door Alarms

These are a little handier than bells. They are small devices (usually battery powered) that your hang on a doorknob and emit a loud noise when disturbed. Remember to check "power supply." Are the batteries new?

Panic Buttons

Most of the newer cars these days, including my Ford Taurus, have a "panic button" on the keyless remote. At the first sign of trouble you can hit that button and your car will sound off and its lights will flash. Whoever came up with that idea is a genius.

Roadside Flares

Always get attention and are more effective than waving a flashlight around.

Guns

I am not going to get into a discussion of the pros and cons of carrying a gun here. If you decide to do so, please keep in mind the following (these apply to firearms as well as stun guns): gun laws vary from state to state and even from county to county and city to city. It is illegal simply to drive through some cities with a gun without local registration. Do not carry a gun unless you know how to use it and have experience using it. Never carry a toy gun.

Life Hammer

An important "tool" to have with you is a life hammer. This safety tool will quickly shatter your window or cut seat belts. Heaven forbid you go off the road into water, but if you do and seconds count, this is the tool to have.

Act Smart, Be Safe

While you should be aware or beware of everyone and everything, this does not mean that you should be frightened. Indeed you should always look as if you are in the know and are in control, even if you are in fact lost. There is a difference between looking lost and looking inquisitive. Other advice: look casual, not "easy." And don't wander.

Many single women wear a pseudo wedding band, the rationale being that a husband may be nearby. Also, if approached

A Story about Asking Directions
I wanted to get to the hotel I was staying in the downtown of a certain city. I had asked directions at the state visitors' center on the highway, where a delightful woman gave me directions and some of her thoughts about the area I was going to. She had lived not too far from my destination. This particular day there was alot of construction, the exits had been changed, and there were detours. I proceeded in the direction that I thought would lead me to the hotel, but I knew this was a mistake when I noticed that the skyscrapers of downtown were getting farther away. I soon found myself on the outskirts of an area that looked a bit questionable. At a stoplight, I asked the woman in the car next to mine: "How do I get to street so and so in downtown." "Just keep driving," she said, "straight ahead." I should have suspected something as the young girls in her car started to giggle as the light changed.

"Straight ahead" quickly put me into the wrong neighborhood, and turning around was very difficult because the side streets were very narrow and full of debris. I finally turned around and headed back towards the skyscrapers. I found a gas station and pulled in, but you can be sure I did not get out of my car. I opened the window enough to ask: "wouldn't the street I was on get me to downtown?" Within a short time I was at my hotel.

Fault? Mine because as soon as I saw the construction at the exits, I should have gotten back on the highway, somehow, and gone to the next exit. I should have been more alert and observant when I asked the woman for directions. There were big clues!

by a slightly suspicious person with a question, you can say something like, "Oh my husband knows that. He'll be right here." And then you leave the scene.

Asking Directions

Do not appear desperate or totally unknowledgeable when asking directions; act as if you are asking for a clarification. Also keep in mind that few people give good directions; my favorite person to ask is a policeman or a fireman.

Think about the person you are asking directions from and give him or her the once-over. If they look "lost" for whatever reason, or look belligerent or with a chip on their shoulder, find someone else. Another possibility is to go into a reputable looking store and ask directions from a store attendant. So what if it takes you a few extra minutes. If asking directions while on the street in a new area, a good line is: "My husband is to meet me at Place Street. How many blocks is it?"

If a car or a person (of any age or sex) follows you, change direction right away. Obviously if they continue to follow you get to the closest safe place or preferably stop and call the police on your cell phone. Do not get distracted by a child, an adult or an animal, regardless of appearances. It could be a set-up.

Pre-trip Finance, Health, and Home Security Issues

To maintain your financial health while you're away, it's important to take care of a number of tasks. There are actually two aspects of this: finance and insurance. This is not a part of trip planning that anyone enjoys, but don't neglect to take care of these things. They may save you lots of hardship later on.

Finances

1. If you are lucky enough to be away for more than two weeks or so, keep a list of what bills will need to be paid during that time. Make a record of each payment in case there are any mix-ups. For very important payments (mortgage, car loan, etc.) use the return receipt service offered by the post office. Have receipts sent to your home. You'll probably never need them, but they might save you a lot of trouble later on.

2. If you can afford it, prepay bills that will come due when you're away. REMEMBER: No explanation needs or should be given about paying your bill in advance. Do not write, "I am paying in advance because I am going to be away!" Also, if paying your bills ahead of time, keep in mind that this may affect your trip budget.

3. Be sure your credit card does not expire while you are gone.

4. Always carry a second credit card when traveling. No matter how long you've held your card, no matter how many years it has been trouble-free, no matter what brand of card it is, stuff happens: you forget that large purchase you made just before you left and lose track of your credit limit, or a check gets lost in the mail, or the company fails to process a payment correctly. So *always* carry a back-up credit card.

5. Take a limited amount of hard cash in small bills, and don't put it all in one place. Use personal checks and travelers checks for larger purchases. Don't leave either of these tasks until the last minute. Don't forget to copy the numbers off your travelers checks (make two copies, one for your bag and other in your notebook) in case replacement is necessary.

Insurance

1. Thoroughly review your insurance coverage to make sure that you have adequate coverage while you are away. Go over everything with your insurance agent. Be certain all policies—home, car, life, and health insurance—are up to date and have adequate coverage.

Don't leave this until the last minute, either. If everything is in order, the process should take but a few minutes. If it is not, then you will be very glad you took the trouble to do this. Make sure you have all of your insurance terms in writing, and if you have changed anything before you leave, request a confirmation fax so you have it in writing that all is in order.

2. Be sure there are not any geographical restrictions on your policy. This is especially important for your car insurance. Sometimes policy protection stops at the border, so if you are planning to drive into Canada or Mexico *even for a minute* make sure you are covered. If you have a maintenance agreement for your car, check on what you have to do to get it fixed when you're away from the dealer.

3. Be absolutely sure that no policies come due while you are away. Insurance companies are not very forgiving for missed or late payments.

Before one trip, I prepaid several bills when I returned and was attacking the pile of accumulated mail, I saw a DISCONNECT notice of sorts! "This can't be!" I exclaimed. As I grabbed the phone to call the company, out fell my check. Immediately I called the business office. Of course, the issue was resolved with haste. A new employee had opened my statement with a check and it was not in the exact amount so she sent it back. Apologizes extended and accepted.

Once upon a time, in my predeparture whirl, I forgot to check the expiration date on my credit card. Usually this is not an issue as new cards are sent out a month or so in advance. I had not given it a thought, except to be sure it was in my pocketbook. It turned out that I had just missed the new card before I left. But I learned my lesson. Keep an occasional eye on the expiration date of your credit card, especially if you are going away.

4. If you are taking any expensive equipment with you (video camera, computer, etc.) make sure that they are covered by your homeowner's policy. You may be able to purchase a short-term policy just for your trip, like what is sold at airports.

5. Put your policies in a safe place. Give copies to someone you trust, just in case! Important papers and documents are valuable. Although most can be replaced, it is a nuisance to do so. So copy them and put important originals away.

6. Remember to take your insurance cards with you, especially for your car and health insurance.

7. Do you have a will? If so, great. If not, draw one up! This is insurance of a different kind. You may think all this is silly, but all you have to do is once go through the problems of a friend who died without a will, and you will get one PRONTO! Not to mention that without a will, Uncle Sam is in charge. Don't get weepy or be bull-headed. You are not in control of your destiny. Just go and get a will made. You can always change it. But you need it while you are on your trip.

Personal Property
In addition to insurance, there are other ways to protect your valuables:

1. Bank Vault/Safe Deposit Box. Wouldn't you rather pay $50-$100 dollars a year to be worry-free and know your valuables are safe? Vaults are in demand. At some banks there is a waiting list. Arrange NOW for the vault even if it is not where your checking account is. A bank vault is a bank vault. Give a family member or a friend a key and authorization to access the box in case anything should happen to you while you are away.

2. Fire Safe Storage Units and Document Vaults. These are usually for large amounts of papers or large photo collections and things of that size. You rent the compartment and supply your own lock. They rent for anywhere from $20 to $100 a month depending on size. I have used these facilities for albums and boxes of photos, children's memorabilia and so on. These are the things that may not be worth lots of money to a thief, but to me they are priceless. I would feel awful if they were lost or destroyed. Those first grade pictures and the outlined tiny hands are treasures—not to mention the collection of baby teeth the Tooth Fairy gave me. These are the special gems that I am some day going to organize.

3. Home Safe. This can be a handy solution, but think if it will really work for you. Can you afford it? Do you have space for it? A medium size home safe is at least $150 and *very* heavy. Where will you conceal it? Closet? Under a table? Who will deliver it and put it where you want it? What exactly do you plan to place in a safe? Is a home safe big enough? Think it through, but a home safe is a good option for many people. Places like Home Depot and Lowe's have a selection to choose from.

Home Security
There are lots of things you should and must do to ensure the security of your home while you are away. These measures are not intended to frighten you, but you must be realistic about the value of your possessions and their increased vulnerability while you're away.

Now that you have decided to take this trip, unless I am very much mistaken, you are going to take many more. A home security system is a great investment. If you do not have one, this is the time to have one installed. You'll probably be surprised how sensibly priced they are and that the monthly fee is a small price for the peace of mind you achieve. Even if it does stretch the budget, go for it.

Once you decide to install a system, call the company of your choice (comparison shop if time permits). Once installed, you will be given window stickers and a yard sign. Place them in prominent spots, as they are (in themselves) a great deterrent to criminals. Be certain the person who watches your house knows the code for the alarm and how it works. Supply the alarm company's phone number and also leave it by the phone.

Home security system or not, there are a few things you should do that are just plain sensible and prudent. Install new bulbs in all security-related lights, such as night lights, outside motion-detector lights, and any light that comes on automatically at night. If someone is checking your home you probably do not have to change all the bulbs, but do be sure to keep new ones on hand and accessible, so if one needs to be replaced it is easy to do so.

Leave a flashlight out for whoever is watching your house. Don't forget to let them know where it is. Don't let your home appear abandoned. The last thing you want is for a home to look like you're away.

Nonetheless, a skilled burglar might figure out that you're away. So put yourself in the mindset of a burglar. What will make a burglar think it's worth the risk for him to break in? He figures you have the usual things, but he doesn't need to have a view of all of your possessions. Check your house outside and inside. Walk around your house—both in daytime and night time—and ask yourself these questions: What do you see? What is exposed? Do you advertise your possessions, or are you discreet? Do the curtains close completely? Do not suddenly change the positioning of your curtains or blinds. Close them a few weeks (if possible) before you plan to leave, so their positioning looks natural and normal. Are there any tempting items in view? If so, remove them.

Special Concerns
1. Sliding glass doors. These are especially vulnerable to burglars and so need extra locks. Use a wooden pole from an old broom, or a wooden closet dowel from the hardware store cut to size— or what I've used is a large tension curtain rod. Lay this "lock" in the floor track. It is impossible to open the door. If there is not a curtain or blind that covers the sliding door, consider putting up a temporary one. You can even tack a blanket up or a sheet. For now we are not seeking beauty but security.

Consider putting an obstacle by any door that is not going to be used, or do the hotel room door jam: the back of a chair tilted under the door knob. Very effective.

2. Glass-paned doors. Obviously you can't change the glass panels in doors, and they're usually too small for a person to climb through. But glass lights and panes are conveniently placed (for the burglar) and if broken can easily be used to reach inside to the door knob. Deadbolts are essential on this type of door. Remember to have them placed away from the glass. And make sure long strong screws are used when installing the bolts. You may also consider deadbolts on solid doors for extra security.

3. Use light timers. These are handy items. You can set lights to go on and off at pre-set times. They are available at many stores for under $10. Use more than one whenever possible. But remember: If a burglar is watching your house (heaven forbid) and sees a repeated light pattern and no real life activity, you are announcing "Hey! I'm away!" So be sure to use the timers when you are at home so an established pattern is set. Don't use them only when you're away. Timers with random settings are an excellent and a preferred choice.

4. Leave on radios and televisions. This uses up a small amount of electricity but gives a house a lived-in feel. You can also use the light timers on these appliances.

5. Fax. Some people turn their fax machines off. If you do leave yours on, put in a new roll of paper.

6. Telephones. Check all your phones and replace batteries in any cordless phones.

7. Unplug computers and printers. After you have saved and/or backed up all of your files, of course. Surge protectors alone may not save your machines from a power surge; many are designed to work just once (sort of like a fuse).

8. Answering machines. If you decide to leave this on, make sure your outgoing message does *not* say that you are away. It is best to leave a simple message saying that you'll get back to the caller as soon as you can. Rewind the tape if necessary. Don't forget your remote access code, so you can check your answering machine when away. Make a copy of the remote operating instructions with your access code to take with you. Many frequent travelers use the voice messaging service operated by the phone company. It is quite reliable and if something goes wrong it can usually be fixed from the road.

9. Deliveries. Make sure that all deliveries are suspended while you are away. Nothing says "This person is away!" louder than a pile of newspapers at the front door. I simply cancel the newspaper. Do not provide a return date. I usually say: "Just a few days. I'll call you when I know." Have someone check and remove any UPS or other package deliveries that are made while you are away. I don't even like to notify the post office, but that is your choice. I just prefer to have my mail taken in by a friend. Leave a basket or some sort of receptacle for the mail. If I am not going to be gone too long, I simply have the mail dropped in the door mail slot. However, security system owners beware: sometimes the noise of something falling on the floor will set off the alarm. It's a good idea to test this before you leave. Remember: A full mailbox is a dead giveaway that your house is unoccupied. Have whoever is looking after your place, remove the mail daily and put it inside your house.

10. Service people. If you have service visits regularly scheduled—like cleaning, yard work or maintenance—be sure to have these visits suspended while you are away. You don't want people nosing around your property, and you don't want to have to pay for a service that might not have been performed.

11. Carport. If you have an outdoor parking space or a carport, ask a friend or neighbor to park a car there while you're away. A continually empty spot is a sure clue that someone is out of town.

12. Trash. The absence of trash is another indication that no one is home, so ask a neighbor to fill your trash can and put it out for collection on pick-up day.

13. Unplug everything that you can. Fans, toaster ovens, toasters, TV, lamps, telephones, clocks. Many house fires start in these small appliances. Unplugging is especially important for computers and electronic equipment that can be damaged by a sudden power surge.

And don't forget those you share your house with:

14. Plants. There are "automatic" watering devices for plants, which are handy, unless you have a jungle or are going to be away for a while. Otherwise, you'll need to ask someone to take care of the plants while you're away. If you have plants all over your home, you might consider putting them in a group and leaving jugs of water by the plants. Even if you leave plants in separate areas of the house, make it easy and leave convenient bottles of water near by. Clean, prune, mist, water your plants. You might also want to feed your plants before you go away—the plants like this.

15. Animals: As important as pets are, it's hard to imagine that anyone would actually forget to have them taken care of when leaving town. And there are so many different animals and ways to handle them that I won't discuss that here. I'll just urge you not to leave it until the last minute. This is one of the first things to deal with before you go, and one of the few problems that could completely derail a planned trip.

Into the Home Stretch: Finalizing Packing

By now, all of your belongings have been divided into categories and are in their respective boxes. You have a number of plastic boxes of various sizes placed somewhere in your home. The hardest part of packing—choosing your clothing—is about to begin.

First, let me editorialize a little: I think it's important to dress nicely when you travel. That doesn't mean fancy, and it doesn't mean expensive. You can have style without money. It costs nothing but a tiny bit of your time. It doesn't take much longer to put on a pair of nice pants versus sloppy pants. There are many reasons for this: dressing well gives an appearance of knowing, which gives you an aura of assuredness and confidence. This is very important for women travelling. Also, your clothes represent who you are. Clothes are the first thing people will notice about you. And besides, I've always found that if you look good, you feel good. So dress nicely, but do not draw attention to yourself.

Your Travel Wardrobe

With your day by day schedule in hand you are going to plan and anticipate weather conditions, dress options, etc. while you are adventuring. The Weather Channel (and its web site) and the *USA Today* weather map are very helpful.

List what you will realistically need each day and for each night!

DAY 1:	NIGHT 1:
DAY 2:	NIGHT 2:
DAY 3:	NIGHT 3:
ETC.	

If you are visiting a friend, you might ask if there is something on the agenda for which you might need a special outfit. Here are some general rules about what to take and what to leave behind:

1. Don't be fabric foolish: Dark colors and some polyesters and synthetics retain heat. In 100 degree temperatures the fabric

---

TO THOSE THAT ARE GIVEN, MORE IS EXPECTED

—well-known quote

Keep a running list of all of your clothing items, and keep a copy in your travel notebook for those important surprise thoughts and additions. Like suddenly you remember the top or shirt you haven't worn for ages that would be just right for your trip (if you can find it)!

you're wearing really makes a difference! Cotton materials are *cool*—especially 100% cotton. Light colors or wonderful whites are usually the coolest. They may get dirty faster but you'll be more comfortable. Also if you are wearing a shirt, tie its tails together at your waist, not stuck in your skirt or slacks. It is a neat look and eliminates one more layer of clothing near your derriere.

As popular as t-shirts may be, they can be hot with the standard high neckline, even if they are 100% cotton. Open neck shirts are cooler.

2. No tight-fitting clothing: It's very important to feel comfortable when travelling and driving. Tight-fitting clothing is not good for one's circulation, and that is especially true for your undergarments and shoes. For driving I recommend light fabric slacks with possibly a drawstring or elastic waist, and a long sleeve starched cotton shirt. A light fabric shell is good to have on, as you can open the shirt and wear jacket style.

3. Layering is important: In some places, especially in the West, mornings can be very chilly, but by 11 AM it warms up considerably. On cold mornings you may want to start with a sweater and a jacket and perhaps a hat, gloves and socks. Have comfortable clothing on underneath for when it warms up and the upper garments can be taken off.

It is 110 degrees and you are stopping to take a picture of a blooming cactus, or you are in the Badlands and you decide to get out and sit and contemplate. If you don't have a collared shirt on (with long sleeves), then put on the "spare" white shirt that you have kept easily accessible. Otherwise, the sun will find you and your neck and your arms.

4. Take starched cotton shirts: Heavy starched shirts look better, feel better and stay looking better longer. The sleeves are a little stiff to roll up the first time. You will be delighted how cool a starched cotton shirt can be. Starched shirts (I have each put on a separate hanger, in separate plastic bags) take up hardly any room if you lay the shirts flat in the back of your car or in the trunk. I keep within reach a white cotton long sleeve man's shirt to put on instantly if necessary. The neck collar on a man style shirt can be turned up to protect your neck from the sun.

5. Take at least one "dress-up" outfit: One of the popular long stretch dresses that can be "gussied up" is ideal! You never know, you might just need it. There are still some places in the world where formal attire is required, and most such places are very, very nice. Don't deny yourself the opportunity.

6. Shoulder pads: a must! Use with your t-shirts, shirts and that just-in-case dress. Everything looks better. Padding does make a difference—for a lot of things!

7. Belts: A stretch belt, an everyday belt, and a nice belt. If desperate you can always use a bungee cord or a piece of ribbon.

8. Slacks: Stick with lightweight and loose. No skin tight! Crinkle light-fabric slacks are ideal. You twist and knot them when you pack and after you wear them. They keep their "look". Loose fitting, lightweight and light colored are the best when driving.

9. Shorts: Proper shorts if the bod and legs are right. No tight fitting shorts that display the backside of your form (regardless of your shape!) *Nothing* up to the water works – regardless of age! You do not want to call attention to yourself for any reason.

10. Scarves: A trademark of mine. Take all sizes and fabrics and colors. There are a zillion ways to use a scarf: around your neck, your head, your hair, as a belt, over your shoulders, or on your bag as an accent. Take a very large one and tie it around your hips as a bathing suit cover-up or a sarong. Be creative and have fun with your scarves. Buy some as you travel that are indicative of a specific area. They are great souvenirs and presents.

11. Shoes: Comfort is the key! Think about where you will be walking: streets, dirt paths, cobblestones, cement and sand. Think about it. Plan your shoes. Break in your new shoes *before* the trip by taking some long walks in them—not just around on the carpet. Take enough shoes that you can give your feet a change every day. What shoes to pack: walking shoes (at least two pairs, preferably rubber-soled), sneakers, sandals, and a pair of nice day shoes. Optional items might include dress shoes or boots.

12. Pocketbooks: For travelling, I prefer a medium-large, deep, lightweight shoulder bag with zipper pockets inside and out as my carryall pocketbook. Sometimes I will put a real pocketbook *inside* the carryall bag. The ideal outer bag has a broad zip top. The result is a double bag. I carry it over my shoulder. I confess this can get a little heavy, but I have everything with me, and I know it's safe. I am sure to *never* put it down unless I put my foot on it or through the strap. Another way to carry pocketbook items is to categorize them in individual baggies. Just don't have too many baggies to have to rummage through. Always try to eliminate the clutter in your carry bag so that you always have easy access to whatever you need.

Don't have all your money or all your credit cards in one place. Have only enough money for immediate purchases. Don't use large bills. Have your immediate monies and one credit card easy to get to, perhaps in a deep outside pocket of your outside bag. A small baggie is ideal to put these in. You can safety pin increments of dollar bills at different places in the bottom of your pocketbook. Some women pin cash (paper bills, that is) inside their blouses or bras for very safe keeping. Loose change is heavy. Don't let it accumulate. Keep in a handy plastic bag or small light change purse for easy access.

Always keep your pepper spray very accessible, in your outside pocket or in an outside pocket of your bag. The same goes for a small flashlight, which you may need for security (or reading a menu in a dark restaurant) as well.

For more elegant engagements with that black stretch dress you may prefer to have a smaller pocketbook, but one that's big enough to take your essentials/valuables with you. DO NOT leave valuables of any varieties even hidden in your room. I prefer to take them with me but valuables (if not with you) should be placed in the hotel or an in-room safe if possible. If you use a hotel safe, don't advertise what you are putting in it. Put it first into a nondescript envelope.

Waist packs, backpacks and fanny packs are popular and useful alternatives to a traditional pocketbook. If you decide to use one, think about the position you will wear it in. If it is in the back you can be looking intently at something while someone else is "visiting" inside your backpack. Wear packs with very secure closure, and limit the access by safety-pinning or locking the opening. There are waist packs that have a steel "belt" that secures it and keeps it from being cut away. A money belt is another secure alternative. An excellent source for these and various travel supplies is Magellan's (1-800-962-4943).

13. *Jewelry:* no gems, not even fake ones! They can look very real. Funky, not valuable, jewelry is the *only* kind to travel with. This is the perfect time to wear that offbeat jewelry you purchased. You know what I mean: you can't remember where or why you bought it, but you just had to have it at the time.

Regardless of your pocketbook of choice, never put it down! Keep it securely closed and skin-close to your body. If you are sitting down, and you place the bag on the floor, put your foot through the handles. The head security guard at the Chicago Hilton once told me how important it is for women to be on guard all the time not only about themselves but their belongings. Some women will sit their pocketbook on the floor by their feet or at the side of their chair, but someone may be watching! At the next table there might be a person with a long wire up his sleeve. When the woman is engrossed in conversation, out comes the wire, and away go her bag and the thief.

If you *must* wear a good luck ring or a tiny necklace or pin, go ahead if it makes you feel better. (Linus never let go of his blanket!) But if the ring has a stone of any kind, get in the habit of turning your ring around, so the stone is towards the palm of your hand. Tape it if necessary. Also pendants should hang in the back, not front

14. Rain gear: A rain poncho with hood, and an umbrella. If you don't take them, it'll probably rain your whole trip. Keeping a couple of heavy duty garbage bags with you is a good idea, for unexpected showers (punch holes for head and arms) or for sitting on damp or dusty places.

15. Keep your clothes fresh: They make you feel fresh, not just in hot weather but all weather. Try not to wear the same thing two days in a row. Let items air out after wearing them.

> At the laundromat in spectacular Estes Park, Colorado, I met three young boys from Scotland. They were so excited to be travelling around the USA. They told me where they had been and their thoughts about the places. I told them about some other spots that they might like to visit. Their enthusiasm was so refreshing. It made me pround of our country, not to mention the wait for my clothes went very quickly.

If you're going to be gone for only a week or so, you can take enough whites and light colors to last through your trip. If you are going for longer, then you'll probably have to do a serious wash along the way. That means in a real washing machine, which means in a laundromat. Don't be put off by laundromats. They're a great place to meet people and broaden your horizons.

16. Laundry bag: This can be a pillow case or a heavy duty plastic bag. Do not put your dirty dusty clothes back in your travel bags. You do not want the essences of 100 degree heat or dusty sites mingling with your fresh clothes.

17. Blanket and large towel: Use to cover up things in your car or you, when you take a nap.

Last Minute Considerations

House presents. If you are visiting a friend or friends don't you want to take a house present? Get it before you leave and have it with you. You can gift wrap it now, or if you prefer take the paper and ribbon and wrap as needed.

Clean out the fridge. If you are going to be gone for any length of time, use up perishables and frozen foods before leaving. Leave just a couple of frozen items for that first night and the next morning when you return home. Place an open box of baking soda in both the refrigerator and freezer to absorb any lingering odors. If your ice maker does automatically shut off when full, turn it off manually anyway.

Clean house. Put air fresheners around your home. Fluff, place upside down, and turn over all pillows on your sofa and chairs. While away it is a good time to let the pillow stuffing become "uncrunched." Put fresh sheets on your bed and clean towels in the bathroom. You can do this the day before you leave. It is nice to come home to a clean, orderly house.

Empty and wash out all garbage cans.

Empty the dishwasher and clothes dryer. And of course don't leave any wet clothes in the washing machine or leave the house with the washer still running. Remember to leave a little detergent for that first wash when you return.

Turn off outside water. But only if you are traveling in winter.

A Final Checklist (Including, But Not Limited To, The Following):

___packing complete
___house cleaned
___dishwasher and dryer empty
___space heaters, fans, and other appliances unplugged
___home notes out for caretaker
___final bags packed and by the door
___coolers and cups in the car
___ID cards and clue cards in car
___pocketbook packed with requisite cash and travelers checks
___passport (if needed)
___medicines
___cell phone(s)
___camera and film
___notebooks
___set light timers
___water plants
___check windows and doors
___set thermostat
___check oven

Two

ON THE ROAD

Know where you are going and be on your way
—GHD

GETTING DIRECTIONS

As previously discussed, one must always "consider the source" in obtaining directions. The maps and directions on several web sites for example, will get you there—eventually. Often such programs will not recommend the shortest possible route or completely overstate the drive time to get to your destination. The one advantage to this service, though, is that you can print out the actual maps with a printed narrative of the directions.

In any case, always know where you are going before you leave and be sure to write down directions and keep them handy. Even if you have a Ph.D. in cartography you couldn't possibly keep all that information in your head.

Directions to hotels and motels can be obtained by calling their toll-free numbers. Usually the person giving you the directions, however, will be reading the printed directions that they have been given. To veer from their script can cause confusion for them and you. If directions are not clear, call again or ask for the manager. The person at the toll-free number giving you the directions is not typically at your destination anyway. Even if it costs a phone call, call directly to the hotel. It is better than getting lost.

Get all directions before leaving. Make two copies, one for your travel book and one to go in the car—just in case.

MEMOIRS, MEMORIES, AND MEMORABILIA

In addition to taking pictures and collecting memorabilia, maintaining your trip diary will be an excellent way to relive the memories of your journey. I place one of the photocopies of planning maps inside my diary, which is usually a three-ring notebook or photo album with plastic sleeves to protect papers. On the map, which I have marked with the routes that I will be taking, I number the places I visit and make corresponding notes about the places on a separate sheet of paper.

Small file cards slipped into photo pockets work nicely, too. You can keep several such cards in your purse for those spur-of-the-moment anecdotes.

Each morning get in the habit of writing down where you are, where you are staying, weather, temperature and a morning comment of the day. "Did not sleep very well." Or, "Had a good breakfast and chatted with a couple from Coronado." This should take you all of about 63 seconds.

Each night write observations of the day while they are fresh and vivid in your mind, and put the day's mementos in your book. It is much easier to do it every day rather than to try to catch up later. For one thing, your memory won't be nearly as good. Evening notes might take a little longer than 63 seconds.

I keep manila envelopes in the car for receipts, mileage notations, etc. Every time I stop for gas or to sightsee, I put down the mileage, time, weather and other miscellaneous information. ("I saw a bear!") During the day, wherever you go, save the receipt, a menu, a brochure or any little thing. They will brighten and jazz-up your diary.

You will of course want to have a decent camera with you, either the traditional film variety or one of the fancy digital machines. The advantage to digital (on the more high-end models) is that you can view your pictures right away (though one at a time on the back of the camera) and even download them to a computer and e-mail them to friends. However, digital cameras are expensive and not much fun unless you have access to a laptop or a PC. I use a good old film camera.

You should treat film as you would gas and water: always keep a full supply on hand. You never know when you are going to come across something special and want to shoot an entire roll. You should also consider having a few rolls developed during your trip. For one thing, this could tell you whether or not your camera is working properly. (I once shot an entire roll with a stuck shutter, so I know of which I speak.) One very reliable place to have your film processed is Walgreen's drug stores, of which there are some 4,000 across the U.S.

Some people forego a camera altogether and just purchase postcards—not to send, but to put in their diary or photo album. Postcards are certainly less expensive than taking fourteen pictures of the same spectacular sunset, and the quality is better. For sending postcards, you might consider making address labels before you leave. Be sure to send cards—even if you just write a "HI" or the weather. You like to receive cards. Send cards!

A video camera is another excellent way to document your trip, but always remember to take extra tape and keep that battery charged.

Another option is to purchase a small tape recorder. The expense is about $30.00 and you can record your thoughts, observations and experiences as you go. There only drawback is that you will have to transcribe your tapes at some point, unless you are in love with the sound of your own voice.

If you plan on taking any high-priced equipment, make certain that it is covered by insurance while you are on the road.

CAR SAFETY

Getting Gas
Getting gas is something you already know how to do, but I have a few tips that apply especially to travelling on your own.

Never let your gas tank fall below a quarter full. Ever. The gauge goes faster from the quarter mark to empty than it does from full to three-quarters full. Be alert and watch the gas gauge. It's easier than you think to run out of gas. This is not something you want to discover at any time, much less after dark. As sure as water is wet and gas has fumes, letting your gas gauge fall below a quarter full is certain to eliminate any sign of a gas station for miles. When you're desperate and frantically looking for gas—that's when you see a tiny sign for a gas station. Hallelujah! Then you pull in and find the station is closed because a carnival is in town and everyone is there.

I've driven countless miles, and I've learned the hard way. On three occasions the "low fuel" light has gone on, always in the middle of nowhere. It was a sickening feeling. I had just not paid attention.

Gas stations are usually easy to find, but *never* assume that there is an open gas station *just ahead*. Sometimes they are closed, sometimes they are far from the highway. Eventually, of course, you'll find one. If you follow the quarter-tank rule, you'll find it before the tank is empty.

By the way, one of my favorite places for gas is Truck Stops of America. They are always open and you will find lots of people there and a well stocked store for various car gear and food.

Octane. The gas distributor recommends one octane. The owner of the station says another. The car dealer says yet another. I use only High Test in my car because I think and feel that it might help to keep the engine cleaner. I don't mind the few extra cents per gallon. Check your owner's manual for the recommended gas octane for your car.

Getting Gas. Here are a few precautions to remember when you are on the road traveling.

Always fill up at a well-lit and busy station.

> WHEN GETTING GAS:
> Close all windows.
> Turn off AC or Heat.
> Turn off lights.
> Turn car off.
> Take your keys, one credit card, and the pepper spray.
> Do not leave your pocketbook open and in view. Put it on the floor under a towel.
> Lock doors.
> Pump gas.
> Clean windows if necessary.
> Pay with credit card, preferably at the pump.

Do not set things on top of your car

You may not realize it, but you have a lot more on your mind than you realize and *forgetting* is too easy. If you place something on top of your car, don't be surprised if you forget it and never see it again. It's in a ditch somewhere or flattened in the middle of the road.

If you have to go into the store, move your car closer to the store, not only for your protection but also for someone else who might need the gas pump. Never leave your car unlocked or windows even a tiny bit open, even if you are relatively close by. It is truly best to keep your car locked *always*.

Necesssity stops should only be made at reputable places. Do not leave your bag in the car. Park your car in front of or as close to the place as possible. Take your pocketbook with you. Lock your car. Don't dawdle. Don't put your bag in front of you on the floor; put it on a hook if possible.

DOS AND DON'TS OF HIGHWAY TRAVEL

Speed limits on interstate highways vary from state to state, so be aware of possible changes as you cross state lines. If you have cruise control, use it. It will not only help you maintain the legal speed limit but will also allow you to move your feet around, making for a more comfortable drive.

In rural areas be aware of animals wandering onto the road. Don't take those "Deer X-ing" signs lightly. Hitting any animal is not pleasant, but hitting a big animal is like hitting a brick wall. People have totaled their cars in collisions with large animals. Not to mention human damages.

If you're tired, stop and take a nap. Even a short one does wonders. It's far better than falling asleep at the wheel and waking up in some strange hospital (or not waking up at all). I recommend taking a small, airline-sized pillow with you. I use a buckwheat pillow that cozies around my head and neck and is not too big. Of course, if you do stop try to find a secure rest area where there are plenty of other people around. And lock yourself in your car.

Try not to be a Good Samaritan, or at least do so in a way that will not put you in harm's way. If someone waves to you, pay no attention. If they are pointing at something on or in your car, pull off at the next service or rest area and check. Do not pull onto the shoulder and get out of your car. If you must pull over, lock the car and call the police *immediately.* Do not get out of your car. If someone else needs help, call the police from your cell phone.

If you need to get something out of the cooler, use the cell phone, or whatever, leave the highway carefully, signaling in advance. Slow down, but relative to the traffic in your lane. Pull over as far as possible on the shoulder of the road. Hopefully, you will not have to get out of your car. When returning to the highway, stay on the surface road until you have attained the appropriate highway speed to readily get back into the traffic flow of the highway.

Keep track of where you are at all times. If you do need to call for help, the first thing you will be asked is: where are you? An inexact answer is not helpful. As you drive, keep track of identifying markers, such as road signs, mile markers, billboards, exits. This is not as easy as you think, especially in rural areas where the landscape may not change a whole lot for tens of miles.

Never try to read a map while driving. Pull over to the side of the road. It's not worth risking an accident to save a few seconds of driving time.

If the light turns yellow, stop. There are automatic cameras at many intersections. Don't run red lights. It's not just unsafe; you'll probably receive a very expensive portrait of yourself and your car in the act.

Avoid aggressive drivers. Do not be intimidated or angered. Don't let gestures, eye contact, or discourteous driving effect you. Do not return glances or gestures. Get out of the way of dangerous drivers.

Leaving Your Car

When stopping to eat, shopping, or to take in an attraction, try to park close to other people and their cars. Do not pick a spot that is either isolated or hidden from view. Always lock

---

I once had tire trouble on a fairly empty stretch of an Interstate in Kentucky. I needed help and called the police:

Me: Officer, I need help. I have a flat tire.

Officer: Lady, where are you?

Me: Officer, I pulled off on the frontage road.

Officer: Are there any signs around? Do you remember the last exit?

Me: I think I saw a billboard about a restaurant.

Officer: Lady what was the last exit you remember and how long ago was it?

Me: Not very long ago. There was a town with lots of industrial smoke stacks.

Officer: Lady, stay in your car. Lock the doors. We will find you. The last exit was probably Kingsbridge.

Me: Yes. That was it . . . I think.

"I'm at ..."

your car, and shut the windows all the way. If you have pulled over for a cat nap, park at the end of a full area of cars. Check cars on either side of you.

Alarms and Clubs: Today most cars come with an alarm. My Taurus has an anti-theft system. They are useful, but not nearly foolproof. Have you ever noticed how little attention is paid to car alarms? Alarms don't stop a fast thief from breaking into your car. Nothing is foolproof, but a "Club" or similar device is a good deterrent. It takes about 30 seconds to put a club on, and though it won't stop a determined car thief, it will at least slow him down.

Don't look like an unwitting traveler. You may have out of state license plates, but you don't have to look like you don't know the area. Keep travel gear, such as maps, hidden.

Be especially careful in parking garages. Try to park near an attendant's station. I don't care how many surveillance cameras a garage has, I am very much on alert when going into a garage—any garage—day or night. The surveillance cameras are not closely monitored like Houston's mission control. They may not even be on. So you must always be alert and aware in a garage.

When exiting or approaching your car, look all around. Look up. Look down. Look under. Have your pepper spray ready. If you don't feel comfortable, don't go to your car *alone.* Trust your intuition. Ask an attendant or security guard to accompany you.

If you have an alarm on your car keys, keep your finger on it. Don't hesitate to use it.

Luggage security. The Taurus station wagon has a shade that you pull across the back area of your car to "hide" things. This should be pulled up all the time. I also put nondescript items such as my starched shirts or a blanket over valuables. In a sedan, luggage is of course secure in the trunk, but if you have anything in the back seat cover it in a similar fashion. My older son reports that he saw a clever idea for protecting items: A metal dog kennel was used to put the bags in and then it was locked.

FOOD FOR THE ROAD

With respect to food, there is one general common-sense rule to follow when you are traveling: eat less. Keep in mind that you will be sitting for long periods of time, and that you don't want to feel bloated. Also, being a little bit hungry will help you stay alert and stave off any drowsiness. If you have wanted to lose weight, this is a good time to do so.

Stay away from fatty, greasy, salty and sugary foods. Drink sweet and caffeinated beverages only in moderation. Dilute soft drinks. You will be surprised how refreshing they are this way and not so sugary-filling. Dairy products and hot weather do not always go together well, so in hot climates stick with water and very lightly flavored beverages.

Keep your meals simple and small. For breakfast I recommend three small items, such as juice, coffee, and a muffin. Try eating a small lunch as well. I often get the child's meal. It is just right. I also tend to eat an early and light dinner. If I am spending the night in a motel and getting up early the next day and adventuring on, then I really like to eat in my room, relax and go to bed relatively early.

Do not take a lot of food in the car. You will have the tendency to nibble and munch all day. You'll end up stuffing yourself with junk, and then not feeling like eating out, which is one of the best parts of travelling! Some good car foods include spray cheese, crackers, peanut butter, dried and fresh fruit, granola bars, instant coffee or tea, and water, water, water.

It's always nice to have some ice on hand, but if you do not like it skating around the bottom of your cooler, or turning your food soggy, place it in two zip lock bags or a wide mouth thermos.

Do not chew on ice or bite hard on a carrot or such. You do not want to break a tooth a thousand miles away from your dentist.

On long drives munchies are fine as long as they are sensible munchies. No salty or greasy chips or heavy candy bars. A piece of fruit, an all natural lollipop or . . . surprise: a bag of crisp chopped lettuce, kept cool next to your baggie of ice.

FINDING YOUR LODGING AND CHECKING IN

When you call the place you've chosen, be sure to find out *exactly* where it is located. If it is just off the Interstate and can be seen from the highway, good. If not, then find out exactly how to get to the front door. At major exits—let us use the Brunswick, Ga., exit as an example—there are many motels with their neon logos sticking up in the air. You can see that they are "there" but no yellow brick road leads you to their door. Because so many motels are close together and some set back, the road to the entrances are not always clear, so be alert and careful.

On checking in, you may be given an electronic "key" in a small folder on which your room number will be written. Hopefully the clerk will point to your room number, never saying it for wrong ears to hear. Likewise, you do not announce your room number. If necessary, the clerk can give you a map showing where your room is located. When you go to your room, if *anything* looks wrong, pick up the phone immediately and call the front desk, or leave the room and speak with the front desk clerk. Motel personnel more than understand travelers' concerns and try to help.

Keep your car key alarm next to your bed. If for any reason you need assistance, push your key alarm. Unless your car is parked very far away the alarm will sound, summoning someone—as well as waking up a few people. I always try to park my car as close to my room as possible.

Park your car either close to your room or close to the motel's entrance. I put a Club on the steering wheel and cover it with the large towel or blanket. Be sure all items are covered.

Just outside Deadwood, S.D., I spied a little shopping strip. I went into the small dress store called "Maurices" with a sale sign in the window. Of course I had never heard of Maurices, but there is a special force that attacks me whenever the magic word sale is close by. Hanging on the sale rack were several items that obviously had been purchased for Prom Time. There outside of Deadwood, South Dakota, I found a velvet evening gown, reduced, the right size . . . and by a most upscale popular designer of the day! Needless to say, I kept my eyes open for the next Maurices . . . and I have found several.

Near the front desk, there is usually a rack of brochures about local and nearby sights. These are good to take and possibly consider doing or save for info for the next trip. Local real estate guides are free and provide an interesting perspective on the area as well.

Hopefully you will have only one or two bags to bring in and possibly your laptop computer.

If you are going to go out for dinner, then plan accordingly. Remember you are in a strange area. No night exploring. If you arrive in town, and it's still light outside, take a little tour of the town. Drive to the main shopping area, explore a little, pick out a place for dinner, drop off your film at Walgreen's, whatever. This will give you a sense of the town and its people. Get gas and clean your windows and do any car-fixing that has to be done. Do it now rather than in the morning when you should be on your way.

If you do go out to dinner on your own, be sure to be seated smack dab in the middle of the dining room, not sheepishly off to one side. Take a book, newspaper, or postcards to write, and be prepared to strike up a conversation with the people next to you. Look confident and in control.

If you don't have time or the energy to look around (or if it's after dark) then consider getting dinner to eat in your room. Remember: you want a very good night's sleep, so be careful what you eat and drink.

If you want ice or something from a vending machine, take the key to your room and lock the door. Never, ever go even three steps from your door without locking it. The hallway may look empty, but who knows what will appear when you leave your room?

Other Security Tips

Don't put a sign on the door requesting maid service. This is like announcing that the room is empty! When leaving the room, put the Do Not Disturb sign on the door. You might also want to leave the TV on.

If you go for a swim or to exercise, don't leave your key or any valuables exposed.

Always use the front door of the hotel, even if it's a bit of a hike.

If you ever do need help, yell "Fire!" Statistics show that "Fire" attracts more attention than "Help."

OTHER FEMALE RULES TO FOLLOW (AND NOT JUST WHEN TRAVELING)

Don't do anything to attract attention.

Speak with authority.

Don't talk about what you *have* anywhere, not even what might be in the car, or purchases you have made.

Don't try to impress in any way.

Don't wear that teeny-weeny bikini, the too-short skirt or shorts, or the too-tight blouse.

Don't walk around as if you are on parade.

Don't flirt or flaunt.

Don't make eye contact but do keep your eyes open.

However...

Enjoy the Evening
If this is your first evening in a motel by yourself, you might feel a bit antsy. This is natural, so take the time to get accustomed to your temporary home. Soon you will begin to feel calm, relaxed, and not just adventurous, but *very* adventurous. Remember:

Gerry's night rules:

Take time to think of those precious to you.

Think of all that you have to be thankful for.

Reflect on your past. Learn from it.

Forgive others. Forgive yourself.

Realize YOU are growing with wisdom, abilities, honesty and love.

Think of the future. Anticipate it with joy and integrity.

Respect and admire yourself.

Promise not to say "I can't" only "I'll try."

Apply the golden rule. (Even when driving!)

Pray.

Have a good night's sleep.

Lock your door
Put bells on the door (if you want)
Put a chair under the doorknob
Wedge the alarm under the door
Stretch a bit
Get comfortable from head to toe
Turn on TV—Check out the local news
Write in your trip diary
Bathe, soak, wash your hair
Get settled. Read the paper. Do your nails, order a movie
Call your children—or parents or a friend. THIS IS A MUST.

Just a short while ago, you were wondering if you would take a trip. Look at you now!

In the Morning
If your hotel breakfast is complimentary, for goodness sakes, don't pack a doggy bag. It appalls me that some people see

Free Meal and they think it means they are entitled to take enough for an ocean voyage. If everyone did that, then the complimentary breakfast may become a thing of the past. Be considerate! The management usually won't mind if you take a beverage with you or even fill a small thermos, but it's always best to ask first.

Complimentary breakfasts are served at most motels nowadays, especially the established chains like Hampton Inns, where the breakfasts are especially good. A number of copies of *USA Today* or the local paper are also made available, and a central TV can be heard in the background. It makes for a rather pleasant way to start the day, and it's a great way to get to know people. You will quickly realize how gregarious people are. You can be too. Don't be a stone-faced, non-communicative, dull traveler. Converse—everyone will enjoy, smile and be sensibly friendly.

Some Observations about Hotels and Motels

Pillows. If you wake up with a headache, it does not necessarily mean that you are "coming down with something." Rather, it could be the result of sleeping on the hotel pillow or blanket. Some pillows are made of foam (not particularly comfortable) and some from feathers and some from a mixture. The pillow stuffing might have caused your headache.

In any case, if you do wake up with a headache, don't immediately start taking a cold medication. Once you get going your headache will probably go away. Cold medicines and driving do not mix well and can be unsafe. I find several very deep gargles with Listerine (straight) and a Tylenol work wonders.

Soaps and other amenities. If you leave behind the soap you have used and such complimentary amenities as lotion or shampoo, they will probably be thrown out, so you might as well take them with you. Many people use these items in their guest baths at home (well, maybe not the soap). I keep a heavy medium sized plastic bag for these recyclables.

SENSIBLE SHOPPING ON THE ROAD

The key to shopping on the road is to not be taken in—either by wily street vendors or your own compulsion to buy something you don't need. Also remember that you have placed yourself on a budget, so don't blow all of your discretionary cash at your first stop. Keep in mind that most vendors or shopkeepers are more than happy to see you part with your money, so buyer beware.

Some of the items I like to buy on the road include scarves, pins (of cities, states, or places), t-shirts, postcards, posters, jellies, salsa, etc.—in other words, souvenirs of places I have been. In collecting such mementos, however, it is important to remember that what looks good in Santa Fe may not look quite the same in your New York apartment, whether it is clothing or a work of art. Will the chili pepper earrings or the cement jackalope have the same aura in Toledo?

Of course, one high-quality item is better than five knick-knacks. You might want to take measurements and some interior photos of your home with you on your trip, in the event that you find something special and want to be certain that it fits—both size-wise and décor-wise. It is also useful to have children and grandchildren's sizes with you.

My car seems to go on automatic whenever it sees the word SALE. I was heading home from a long trip once and my car stopped at a huge sale. I found an absolute bargain. Just what my son and daughter-in-law could REALLY use. Small problem, big size! Four chairs and two ottomans by one of the best outdoor furniture manufacturers in the country. The furniture was light with some good conceptual organization and a lot of bungee cords, up it all went on the top of my station wagon. Off I drove. Thank goodness, the finds were at the very end of the trip.

COMING HOME

You are home. Soon after you have closed the front door, and you set your bags down, you realize you are back in the real world. You are facing a pile of mail, bags to unpack, clothes to wash and your job to get ready for. The Post Travel Blues. Those "blues" are natural but they too are probably mixed with tiny "glad to be home emotions." Don't forget to have a nice dinner with extras—even if it is a frozen dinner. You will no doubt ponder how easy the trip actually was and start thinking about the next trip.

It was, after all, only a drive.

Three

FEMALE FRIENDLY FINDS

PLACES & GENERAL TRAVEL INFORMATION

Highways all look the same on a map, but in reality they are not. There are good roads, there are bad roads, and there are just adequate roads. There are scenic highways. There are long, straight, dull highways. There are roads on high terrain, uneven terrain, and difficult terrain. I call some of these roads brake burners or white-knuckle roads. The following will give you my first-hand impressions of many of our highways and highlights of places visited along the way. The information I have provided is highly selective and not meant to be a comprehensive guide of any sort; as you will see, my preferences run to shopping, nice hotels, spas, shopping, special places to eat, the national parks, and shopping. And the places I herewith recommend all have one thing in common: they are perfectly safe for women to visit and enjoy on their own, so long as one is taking all the normal precautions.

ALABAMA

Alabama is an enjoyable state to visit; the roads are generally good and the people congenial. Birmingham is fairly dense but not difficult to navigate. US 78, a decent stretch of road, leads you out of Birmingham to Jasper (pop. 13,000), where I discovered a shopping Mecca, Bud's Discount Center. The car went on automatic pilot and within a few minutes I found myself in a building the size of an airplane hanger. There was a little bit of everything there, but the big bag of "treasures" I purchased probably totaled all of $25.00.

ARIZONA

One rather dramatic way to enter Arizona in the summertime is to take Interstate 8 from San Diego to Interstate 10 and into Phoenix/Scottsdale, a drive of about seven longish hours on a very straight and excellent highway. Once when I left San Diego the temperature was 71 degrees, but by the time I crossed the border (about 180 miles) at Yuma, Arizona the temperature was a very hot but dry 118 degrees. Interstate 8 from San Diego is a decent road but there are very long stretches without anything but heat, dust and rocks. (Although the formations can be impressive, keep an eye out for falling rocks). Be sure to have water for you and gas for the car. You do not want to be without either commodity—ever! You are definitely in the desert. Also be sure to cream your lips and face as the desert sun will definitely find your face, even in the car.

Possibly the hottest, driest town in the USA is Yuma (those in Gila Bend may beg to differ). Yuma is a real town with a population of about 60,000 where you can stretch, eat, get gas and be hotter than you have ever been. I found a small strip mall where there was a "might find anything" store. I call these stores "gypsy stores" because they are liable to have moved on by the time you read this.

Dateland, Arizona, is just a spot on the map but I did stop there once. The Mini Market sign leads you to a gas station with postcards and trinkets; other visible signs indicate that a restaurant, gift shop, and bus stop all occupy a low one-story building that makes up the rest of the town. The café was very clean and friendly; here you can get dates of all varieties (except the two-legged kind), even a date milk shake.

However, I would be very careful about eating too many dates before setting out for a long drive in the heat.

The next landmark is Gila Bend, whose sign greets you as follows:
GILA BEND
Welcomes You
Home of 1700 *Friendly* People
And 5 Old Crabs. Elev. 737

Gila Bend highlights that I saw included two police cars, lots of closed buildings, and a few food shops.

I was told that the shorter route to Phoenix is to take 85 at Gila Bend north to I-10. I tried this once and it was fine. One can also stay on I-8 to Casa Grande and pick up I-10 north to Phoenix. As always, the time of day and your mindset will determine the route you take.

About forty miles outside of Phoenix there is one of the largest prisons imaginable, as well as a juvenile correctional center. Nearby signs read, "Do Not Stop for Hitchhikers." Hmm.

PHOENIX / SCOTTSDALE

A thriving oasis in the middle of the desert, Phoenix is not difficult to navigate so long as you become familiar with the main thoroughfares.

For women travelers, one place not be missed in downtown Phoenix is **Last Chance**, the discount outlet for Nordstroms. To say you will find unbelievable clothing bargains there is the ultimate understatement. One lady told me: "This has become a Sunday afternoon ritual," as we perused the racks and grabbed items we didn't even know we needed. There I was in 100 degree weather, buying sweaters.

The Arizona Biltmore Resort and Spa is another place not to be missed. Designed by consulting architect Frank Lloyd Wright and opened in 1929, it was later bought by William Wrigley, Jr., who became the sole owner, and for the next 44 years the family owned and operated this unique property. In 1973 the property was sold to Talley Industries. There have been several expansions and renovations to The Arizona Biltmore, but it has always retained its special style. In spite of its size, you will not feel overwhelmed (although more signage would help keep you from getting lost in the maze of corridors). A visit to the spa is a "must," as is a game of chess on the "board" that is impressed into the lawn. The resort has three restaurants: a café for casual healthy eating, a grill, and Wright's, the resort's signature restaurant. I have eaten there and the food and ambiance are exceptional.

Even when the temperatures are soaring and a lot of places are only half full, you will find you are not alone at the Biltmore, which attracts visitors year-round.

The Camelback Inn Marriott, Resort and Spa is very relaxed in a southwestern sort of way. Because of the intense summer temperatures the eating area by the pool is misted to cool down guests, great for the temperature but rough on hair-dos. Many of the accommodations ("casitas") are in fact duplexes, with the bedroom and bath on the loft level and the living room, dining area, and "kitchen" area with powder room on the lower level. An excellent arrangement that I thoroughly enjoyed. The spa here is a delight. Another year-round destination.

The Phoenician and **The Royal Palm** are also worth a visit. The Phoenician is glamorous in an ostentatious way, the Royal Palm more quietly sophisticated. Both merit at least a casual walk-through.

Check the local paper for events and exhibitions at some of the fine museums in the area. Obviously there is upscale shopping in Scottsdale and Phoenix, and just up the road from the Camelback there is a wonderful, have-everything grocery store—AJ's.

<u>**Remember resort rates are really low when the temperatures are really high.**</u>

SEDONA

North of Jerome and Prescott is Sedona, an absolutely beautiful area. Take time to stop, especially at places like Slide Rock, a natural water chute; Oak Creek Canyon; and Red Rock State Park.

JEROME

89A—the road from Sedona and Jerome into Prescott—is definitely a **big white-knuckle** experience. BEWARE! 89A is probably the worst road I have ever been on. Some call this road "drivable," but you have my opinion for whatever it is worth. A better way to get to Prescott is to take I-17 to 69.

Jerome, positioned on a steep hill, was a booming mining town of nearly 15,000 people in the 1880s. In 1918 a fire broke out in the 88 miles of underground tunnels, and soon open pit mining became the norm. However, continual dynamiting shook and cracked the town's buildings so much that the actual town began to shift, the jail sliding 225 feet. (It can now be found across the road from its original site.) By 1953 only 50 residents remained in Jerome, but by the 60s Jerome's renaissance was underway. An artists' colony of sorts established itself, and the stalwart residents joined in rebuilding the town.

PRESCOTT

Prescott is charming, and it is hard not to feel welcome in this rather upscale western town. It boasts ideal, gentle seasons, recreational activities of all types, major cultural events and is home to the world's oldest rodeo as well as Prescott College. There are also wonderful antique shops, craft shops and boutiques. A memorable Prescott experience is an evening gathering in the town square by Courthouse Plaza. One night there might be square dancing, something else another night. You can partake or not. But do attend. It is a very happy time under the huge trees on the square.

FYI: The natives pronounce the name of this town more like *press-kit*.

The Hassayampa Inn is a delight and right on the main street, East Gurley. The Inn is easy to find and central to everything. The hospitality is genuine and the dining delicious in the Three Star Peacock Room. A friend who was with me in Prescott and who is something of a gourmet rates the eggs benedict as some the best she has ever had. For guests there is a complimentary breakfast, although the eggs benedict are not included.

With over 450 buildings on the National Register of Historic Places, there is a lot of history in Prescott. There is "Whiskey Row" directly across from the Courthouse Plaza; the old Hotel St. Michael, a true step back into time; and The Palace Restaurant, with its friendly, western ambience and excellent food.

TUCSON/GREEN VALLEY

Tucson is slightly cooler than Phoenix, but still very much desert. The interstates are excellent and roads well marked. Interstate 19 begins in Tucson and goes through Green Valley and on to Nogales, which is on the Mexican border. Because a lot of the roadways are barren, I would not recommend traveling these roads alone at night. The landscape seems to get an eerie nightlife and personality of its own as you drive this relatively dark and empty highway. I would definitely not recommend I-19 from Green Valley to Nogales at night alone.

Green Valley is a charming, growing, and friendly suburb (sort of) of Tucson. A lot of friendly and savvy people, many retired. There is a freshness and upbeat aura to Green Valley.

A few miles south of Green Valley on I 19 is Amado. If you exit at Arivaca Road you will see a huge, concrete cow's skull that marks the entrance of a cantina, and across the way, the popular and famous **Cow Palace** restaurant. Oh! So western and friendly.

THE GRAND CANYON

Not to be missed on any visit to Arizona is the world's biggest hole in the ground, the Grand Canyon. It is truly unbelievable—277 miles long and 18 miles wide with an average depth of a mile. Because of the shifting light the Grand Canyon is always changing. Each time you look, it is different.

There are many lodges to stay at, but reservations are a must. When I checked in Bright Angel Lodge, I was asked if I would like a wake-up call so I could see the sun rise on the rim the next morning. Of course I did this, and it was well worth getting up for.

ARKANSAS

Besides the highway signs there is another way to tell that you are in Arkansas—the bad roads. Some stretches are just fine, but others are not. Just be prepared to slow down for whatever might present itself.

Interstate 30 will take you from the Texas border at Texarkana to Little Rock.

LITTLE ROCK

The historic **Capital Hotel** in downtown Little Rock is a beautiful property that has been totally renovated. Dining in Ashley's, the featured restaurant at The Capital, is an experience that you should not miss. The attention you will receive will be gracious, and even dining alone you will feel very comfortable. I did.

A unique feature of the Capital Hotel is its oversized elevator. One explanation has it that the elevator was meant to transport both horse and rider to one's room; the more plausible story is that the elevator was designed to accommodate women in their broad hoop skirts. Regardless, the elevator is large—large enough to accommodate lots of female travel bags with or without the horse.

Within walking distance of the Capital are the River Market District, the Arkansas History Museum, and the Chamber of Commerce. A trolley will soon be in service to accommodate visitors.

CALIFORNIA
TAHOE/TRUCKEE

A stone's throw from the Nevada line, these places are beautiful. Truckee is the more real area—not so filled with obvious ego-houses, at least from what I saw, but definitely touristy. It is more a historic town. There was the Hotel Rex whose original sign revealed that "Rooms Steamed Heated: $1.00 up." Also seen: The Hotel Truckee, the Truckee Diner, lots of art galleries and tourist attractions. The drive went by Squaw Valley and beautiful Donner Lake. Heading west I was on I-80. You will go from 8000 feet to 5000 feet. The road is excellent, with fantastic and beautiful trees on each side of a gently winding road.

SAN FRANCISCO

Interstate 80 from the Truckee/Tahoe area takes you right into Sacramento and on into San Francisco. While a decent road, I-80 can be congested—very congested, and there are not a lot of convenient gas stations and food places in stretches.

San Francisco is still a gem of a city, although many years ago when I first visited the place it was less crowded and seemed to sparkle more than it does today. There is plenty to see and do in San Francisco, but remember to bring really good walking shoes (maybe even hiking shoes) as the hills of the city are a challenge. Also remember when parking on a steep down-hill to point your front tires toward curb, away from the curb when parking uphill. This will prevent your car from becoming part of the traffic without you.

San Francisco is pretty friendly, but it is a big town and has some areas, I have been told, that you should definitely stay out of, such as the Tenderloin district and the area south of Mission Street.

There is certainly no problem finding good restaurants in San Francisco; North Beach is famous for Italian food, and of course there is Chinatown for Oriental fare.

San Francisco has four hotels of particular note: **The Ritz, The Mark Hopkins, The Stanford Court**, and **The Fairmont**. The Ritz is, well, ritzy, and if a dinner in the main dining room is not in the budget a small munch in **The Terrace** will do. **The Top of the Mark** at The Mark Hopkins features a bar with a spectacular panoramic view of the city, which you certainly pay for with your pricey glass of Chablis.

A fine hotel that is ideal for the woman traveler is **The Majestic**—small, upscale and friendly. To add to its charm, it is a bit out of "downtown," which is fine. Parking is easy and convenient in their covered garage on the next block. From 4PM-6PM complementary hors d'oeuvres and beverages are served. Some interesting shops are within easy walking distance.

There are several highways south from San Francisco, the most expedient of which (for getting to Los Angeles) is Interstate 5. More attractive alternatives are US 101, which weaves in and out of coastal cities, and the famed Pacific Coast Highway (US 1), a white knuckle road that follows the coastline.

SANTA BARBARA
Right along Route 101 is Santa Barbara, charming, clean, beautiful, upscale, and a bit pricey. The shops are delightful and there are consignment shops worth a snoop. The corporate offices of **Magellan's**, American's Leading Source of Travel Supplies, is in Santa Barbara, along with a large retail store. Worth a visit is the **El Encanto**, a boutique hotel and garden villas and one of the National Trust Historic Hotels. Its setting above the city on the "Riviera" is exquisite. It is small,

but that only adds to the charm. The food is delicious and I found the atmosphere and attendants friendly and helpful.

Traveling south from Santa Barbara one gets back on 101, a pleasant drive. If you get hungry for a good hamburger around Ventura, look for **In and Out**, distinguishable by its primarily white with bright red decor. The hamburgers are made fresh in front of you and are delicious, as are the fries and shakes.

LOS ANGELES

Glitzy and glamorous, competitive and costly, fashions and freeways—that's L.A. The historic **Biltmore Hotel**, built in 1923, is located downtown. Many consider it one of the most beautiful hotels in the area—if not in the entire country. To say that every brick at this fabulous hotel has a special story would be underrating the bricks. Events of every variety—the original Oscar ceremonies, an unsolved murder, the restocking of the Graf Zeppelin's kitchens from those of the Biltmore, movies filmed and TV shows taped are just a few of the things that have occurred at this hotel. If only a third of the 683 rooms could talk! Because of its décor, history, and museum-style exhibits one must allow at least an hour—and it could extend much longer—to tour this property.

Much-touted **Rodeo Drive** in Beverly Hills has recently become more of a mix of varying stores of varying worth. When I was first there a number of years ago, the opulence of its shops could not be denied. But it has changed since Julia Roberts traipsed down the famous drive in *Pretty Woman*. Many of the fancy stores are still there, but so are the same chain stores that you can find in Kalamazoo. Still, it is worth at least a look.

Not far from Rodeo Drive is **The Beverly Wilshire Hotel**. It is a grand hotel where Hollywood's stars and history have filled the property over the years. If you dine there you might wonder about the black dinner napkins. Black dinner napkins . . . of course, so one does not get white lint on his or her clothing.

RIVERSIDE

Fifty-five miles east of Los Angeles, Riverside is the navel orange capital of California, but I also found it charming and friendly.

The Mission Inn on Seventh Street is a most unique structure. Built in 1876, it grew in many different stages and is now the size of an entire city block. The turrets, domes, circular stairs, art collections, bell collection, wedding chapel, and Tiffany windows all evoke a Spanish town. It should not be overlooked in your travels.

Carriage rides around town were available when I was there. Definitely a nice change from the car.

LONG BEACH

Attractive and clean, Long Beach features **The Queen Mary**, permanently docked and serving as a floating hotel (no Dramamine needed). Everything is as it was on the original steamship and it is a wonderful way to combine a ship and hotel experience. There are many places to dine and imbibe on board. The Russian submarine **Scorpion** is docked next to The Queen Mary and is open to the public.

CORONADO

A special island, thirteen square miles dubbed the Crown City. The short bridge trip from San Diego takes you to this refined place. Attractive, clean, pleasant and an absolute delight with practically all types of recreational facilities as well as designated bicycle paths. The weather is about as perfect as it gets. No matter where you are—at the book store, grocery store, drug store, antique shop or wherever, you will receive a friendly welcome. Right in "downtown" on Tenth Street, is **The Summer House: Antiques and Home Furnishings**. The attractive young owner always seems to have a wonderful mix of the unusual and just what you might be looking for. There are several thrift shops in Coronado as well. Plenty of eateries can be found on Orange Avenue, Coronado's "main street." **The Stretch Café: The Healthy Alternative to Fast Food** is very small and cozy and deliciously friendly.

Coronado's landmark is **The Del Coronado**, a rare and extraordinary historic hotel that should not be missed. There is something for everyone here and at every price range. Though colder than one might expect, the ocean is inviting and accessible by a wide and clean beach. Recent renovations have only improved upon the already spectacular features of the "Del," whose history includes a visit from the young Duke of Wales as well as providing the setting for the film *Some Like it Hot*.

Dining at The Del is a treat. **Sheerwater**, the newest restaurant, is oceanfront dining at its best. Dress is casual but "correct," a most pleasant way to eat. A bit more formal is the **Prince of Wales.** If dining does not fit the schedule, try to have a drink of any sort at the **Babcock & Story Bar.** It is a wonderful way to rest and regroup.

Not to be overlooked are the many stores at The Del, a tempting shopping treat.

SAN DIEGO

A large, sprawling city with a historic waterfront area, San Diego is a sightseer's and shopper's delight. **The Gas Lamp** district is trendy and congenial with restaurants and shops lining each side of the street. A thrift shop of merit is there, and the funky, trendy **Horton Mall** is a few blocks away. **The Old Town Trolley** is a pleasant sightseeing experience. **Bazaar Del Mundo** is a festival of shops and restaurants of all varieties easily accessible by public transportation. It is easy to spend the day here, so plan accordingly.

In downtown there is one of the most attractive, cozy, quietly glamorous hotels, **The U.S. Grant Hotel.** With less than 300 exquisitely appointed rooms, the hotel is not over-powering, but a gem with its special use of different woods. And it is convenient to all of downtown.

Another place to stay in the area is **Paradise Point Resort,** a 44-acre facility in a tropical setting on Mission Bay that has recently been refurbished and upgraded. Much to do here, especially for the sports enthusiast.

DEATH VALLEY

A flat, hot drive (approx. 2 hours) from Las Vegas, but one that should not be missed. However, before embarking on a trip to Death Valley be certain to gas up and check all the fluid levels in your car. It might also be advisable to let someone know your schedule. The heat is severe, so take every precaution possible. Have water with you and make sure your cell phone is charged up. But do not hesitate to venture. You will be glad you did.

From the official National Park Guide:

> *Check your car gauges frequently. Radiator water is available from storage tanks along park roads. If you car develops vapor lock, wrap a wet rag around the fuel pump and line to speed cooling. And if your car breaks down, stay with it.*

Death Valley contains hundreds of abandoned mines and associated structures. Many openings have been closed but it will take years to close the rest. Use extreme caution in driving and walking around mines and watch carefully for openings. NEVER enter abandoned mines. STAY OUT and STAY ALIVE.

Austere desert beauty and Borox mines (as in 22 Mule Team) highlight the drive to Death Valley. You will pass **Marta Becket's Amargosa Opera House**, where plays are created and performed by Ms. Becket herself. Her artwork adorns the walls and ceiling of the Opera House as well. Performances are throughout the year, but call for exact days and time.

Death Valley is isolated by nine mountain ranges and is one of the driest and hottest places in the world. Do not remove any rocks, plants or artifacts of any kind as Death Valley is considered an "outdoor museum" and is protected by federal law. The first real sign of civilization is just as you near the "heart" of Death Valley when **The Furnace Creek Inn** suddenly appears like a mirage. In the middle of nowhere you are suddenly somewhere. Though not fancy, Furnace Creek Inn is a charming, AAA three-star property with all the amenities. It is attractive, well appointed and comfortable. When you check in and you realize that the temperature is 110 degrees or more outdoors, the hotel attendant reminds you that even if you sit out in the sun for quite a while (not advised) you will not get a burning tan, because you are so far away from the sun. Most of Death Valley is below sea level. The water in the pool has a velvet consistency—at least to me. The pool is filled with natural spring water and is a fairly consistent 85 degrees.

The wind does blow in Death Valley, especially in December and March. At night the sky is the blackest of black and the stars are so thick and look so low that you feel you could reach up and grab one. Unbelievable!

You cannot be in Death Valley and not visit **Scotty's Castle.** "Death Valley Scotty," Walter Scott was a sort-of con man who convinced Chicago insurance magnate Albert Johnson to back him in his search for gold. Since Albert Johnson and his wife were very much taken by both Death Valley and Walter Scott, they decided to build him a castle with all the trappings, including a huge pipe organ, right in the desert. The castle was taken over by the National Park Service in 1970.

COLORADO
DENVER

The Mile High City is mid-west special, more like a very large town than a big urban center. I stayed at **The Oxford Hotel**, over 100 years old, a place of old world charm on a small scale with only 80 rooms. The Cruise Room, the Oxford's famous art deco bar, serves a delicious Martini as well as a companionable setting. The hotel's Cadillac car with friendly driver is at your disposal at no charge, to chauffeur you to any place within two miles. You can call for the car to come get you when you are ready to return to The Oxford. This is a wonderful service, particularly for women. At The Oxford be sure to ask details about the tunnels that lead away from the hotel, and also the oversized men's "necessities" that are downstairs.

The Brown Palace Hotel is grand, stately, and impressive, displaying both Victorian and Italian Renaissance architectural styles. As you stand in the lobby and look upward to the impressive six tiers of cast-iron balconies, the stain glass ceiling showers the lobby with colors. FYI: Two of the cast-iron panels were installed upside down. Can you spot them?

A free-guided tour from the lobby is given on Wednesday and Sunday at 2:PM. Tea is served in the lobby every afternoon.

Whether staying at the Brown Palace or just visiting the place, you can walk a block over to **The 16ᵗʰ Street Downtown Mall**. Full of shops and eateries, this is the perfect place for a leisurely stroll or some serious shopping.

BOULDER

The drive into Boulder from Denver is scenic and easy, about 45 minutes. Boulder is an attractive university town, full of the activity that its largely youthful population brings. Its dramatic backdrop, the Flatirons, rise to over 8,000 feet above the city, and still farther beyond the snow-capped Continental Divide looms at over 13,000 feet. Cosmopolitan in a relaxed sort of way, Boulder has a little bit of everything.

The Hotel Boulderado [Boulder + Colorado] is a historic hotel in downtown that first opened in 1909. Had you checked in when it first opened the rate would have been from $1.00 to $2.50 a night, depending on room size and conveniences. Visiting this landmark you will feel like you are stepping back in time.

Within a very short walk from the Boulderado is the award-winning **Pearl Street Pedestrian Mall**. Full of boutiques (some pricey) and restaurants, this is a shopper's Mecca. At night, especially in summer, various performers entertain, including a fellow who can guess what neighborhood you live in from your zip code.

Open seasonally and only on weekends, **The Farmer's Market** at the end of the mall offers produce and other items from local gardens and farms.

Near the Pearl Street Mall at 1770 13th Street is the **Dushanbe** [doo-shan-bay] **Teahouse**. Dushanbe, sister city to the "People's Republic of" Boulder, is the capital of Tajikistan. A beautiful structure, it was decorated by more than 40 native artisans over a three-year period. "This is a gift to the people of Boulder to make their souls happy..." Both lunch and dinner are served.

ESTES PARK

Estes Park, the "gateway to Rocky Mountain National Park," is an easy 45-minute drive from Boulder. A beautiful area, albeit a bit touristy in season, Estes Park is home to **The Stanley Hotel**, a magnificent white structure built in 1909 by automobile pioneer F.O. Stanley of "Stanley Steamer" fame. If the building looks familiar, that's because it was the setting for the Stephen King film *The Shining* starring Jack Nicholson. Renovations are being made at The Stanley as I write.

A delicious Italian restaurant is **Sweet Basilico Café**, great food at the right price.

GRAND JUNCTION

I-70 out of Denver takes you to Grand Junction in about 4½ hours. The highway is excellent, and takes you through some of the most beautiful scenery in America. Be advised, however, that winter weather on Vail Pass and the Eisenhower Tunnel can cause considerable delays. A flashlight or two, blankets, a small shovel, and heavy boots are advised for the winter traveler.

Grand Junction and surrounding areas are unpretentious and friendly, until you get into the canyon country, where rock formations are spectacular. I particularly recommend a drive through **Colorado National Monument**, easily accessible from Grand Junction. A convenient place to stay is the

Adam's Mark Hotel, right off 1-70 at exit 31. It has two eating areas, the Observatory Lounge and a fine dining room, Red Cliffs. Women will feel comfortable and safe here.

Palisade is within 10 minutes of downtown Grand Junction to the east along I-70. With all due respect to the Peachtree state, you have not tasted peaches until you have tasted fresh peaches from Palisade. Their taste is very different from the Georgia peach. There are other delicious fruits from the area, so be sure to "fruit-up" for delicious car treats. Don't leave the area without a trip to **Palisade Pride**. Palisade Pride, Inc. takes the area's fabulous fruits, dries them without the use of sulfur or toxic preservatives, and then hand dips them in Guittard Chocolate. Also enjoy a visit to **Enstrom's,** a 50 year old family business famous for their almond taffy.

CONNECTICUT
This small state is a mix of fabulous shorelines, estates, bucolic settings, industrial cities belching smoke, major college campuses, abandoned mill towns, ski areas, and a few unpretentious towns that seem to have bypassed progress. Towns like manicured Greenwich, Darien, and New Canaan are so close to New York City that they take on an almost urban aura, while places such as Salisbury, Lakeville, and Litchfield attempt to preserve their country charm, albeit in a sophisticated way.

There are many ways to get to Connecticut and sometimes the same road has two different names or route numbers. Obviously the roads closest to New York City are going to be hectic, and construction seems to be endless. Once you are in the country road travel is better, although Connecticut is notorious for winding, twisting, hilly roads that seem to lead nowhere. However, they do lead to some charming towns with antique shops, boutiques, yard sales, country auctions, or church fairs.

The coastline has a lot to offer with its charming towns like Madison, Guilford, Old Saybrook and Essex, which is actually on the Connecticut River. I-95 on the weekends in summer can be a parking lot, though, since it carries all the major beach traffic from New York on up to Massachusetts.

DELAWARE
I normally take US 13 to get to Delaware from Virginia, a good (and well-patrolled) road that goes through Laurel,

Seaford, and Harrington before reaching Dover. Antique shops, variety stores, and stands can all be found along US 13, made all the more appealing because Delaware has no sales tax. Right on US 13 is charming **Odessa**, a tiny historic town worth a drive-through. It will not take you very long and it is charming. In December Odessa hosts a Christmas program that includes historic tours.

The newly built Delaware Turnpike, a toll road, is accessible from a number of places, and eventually takes you over to the long and high Delaware Memorial Bridge and onto the New Jersey Turnpike.

FLORIDA
I-95 goes straight down the east coast of Florida, presenting the driver with a "hit parade" of fabulous places to visit along the way.

JACKSONVILLE
Jacksonville is a beautiful city that has improved itself greatly over the years. The city skyline at dawn and dusk is particularly striking, one of the most attractive commercial areas I've been. The riverfront area, **Jacksonville Landing**, is a marketplace mix of restaurants, shops, attractions and other delights.

If you're fan of popular music and traveling through the Jacksonville area, flip to 90.9 on your dial. That's the radio station of Jones College, one of my favorites.

After Jacksonville I tend to stop at the **St. Augustine Outlet Stores** at Exit 95. There is a wonderful Hampton Inn there, complete with complimentary cookies and the outlet is a very short distance, although I would not recommend walking. The Belz Outlet is also there.

Exit 95 also takes you to Old World St. Augustine. Years ago I took my sons here to see **The Oldest Wooden School House**, **Ripley's Believe It or Not**, and of course the famed **Fountain of Youth.** Henry Flagler developed this area and now a special destination resort has capitalized on what Flagler envisioned. The 1888 **Casa Monica Hotel** recreates an era of grandeur in St. Augustine and has been awarded Four Diamonds by AAA. From the time you arrive and give your car keys to the parking attendant, you realize that you are definitely at a female friendly property. Security is excellent; dining is delightful.

If time allows, you might want to take A1A and US 1 for a short time, just to see the area around what used to be *the* road south. (I would not recommend driving this at night, however.) This road takes you through a Florida that you probably won't see featured in the glossy brochures. I nostalgically recall many trips taken with my parents along this route in our Lincoln Zephyr.

Traveling down I-95 you will pass Daytona and Cape Canaveral and other places you may wish to investigate. I find Exit 70 in **Palm Bay** to be an excellent stopping point in the seemingly endless drive from Jacksonville to Fort Pierce; there are a lot of stores of all varieties, and plenty of fast-food places.

VERO BEACH

I know of only of a few places first-hand in Vero, but from everything I have seen and experienced, it is very pleasant and accessible. **Disney's Vero Beach Resort**, where I enjoyed a delicious breakfast, is typical Disney—friendly, clean and well organized. Vero is also home to spring training for the Los Angeles Dodgers, who occupy a complex known as **Dodgertown**. The Vero Beach Dodgers, a Class A farm team, plays all summer long at Holman Stadium.

FT. PIERCE

At Fort Pierce you have the option of picking up the Florida Turnpike (Exit 65), a more direct route and less congested than remaining on I 95. The Turnpike from Ft. Pierce is a toll road, which probably explains why it isn't as congested as I-95. There are gas stations and food courts—and police cars—aplenty.

Ft. Pierce itself offers the usual line-up of fast-food restaurants, but it also has a very good shop, **Boudrias Groves**. Here you can obtain fresh grapefruits, oranges, and other local produce and enjoy a free sample or two. They also have a selection of jams and jellies and miscellaneous Florida souvenirs, including T-shirts. Gas is available here, there is a clean rest room, and the personnel are all very friendly.

WEST PALM BEACH

The Palm Beaches are easy to get to either via the Florida Turnpike or I-95.

The main thoroughfare in West Palm is Okeechobee Boulevard, accessible directly from an exit off the Florida Turnpike. Everything seems to be on or just off of Okeechobee: chain stores, boutiques, car dealers, fast-food places, etc.

A new shopping area, **City Place**, is, as its motto states, "Unlike Any Place." Upscale and very attractive, City Place is actually individual shops arranged in a small-town atmosphere. Every store imaginable is there, and the presentations are most attractive. As we all know, it is not what you do but how you do it, and City Place does it well.

Clematis Street District is more laid-back. It has wonderful shops and great eating places, including **Sloan's Ice Cream Parlor**, where even the rest room here holds a surprise, particularly if you forget to lock the door.

PALM BEACH

There are few places in the world that are like Palm Beach, which is an island of absolute luxury in an absolutely (although slightly unbelievable) beautiful setting. Even the grocery store and post office blend in incognito. One feels safe in Palm Beach and it is friendly, but you may not achieve an immediate warm fuzzy feel because unless you are especially outgoing, you are a stranger in this closely-knit community. While it is not essential, it does help to have a friend from the area with you (and it does help to dress somewhat fashionably so that you don't stick out like a sore thumb).

Worth Avenue, Royal Poinciana Way and everything on the island are delights for female shoppers, so long as you aren't intimidated by a $500 belt or a $1,000 dress. You can always shop with your eyes.

The Breakers Palm Beach ranks among the top resorts in the world. The architecture, décor and attention to detail are all worth a look and, if possible, even an overnight stay. (Check for special rates at *www.thebreakers.com;* some are quite reasonable.) You will not regret it. If a night at this marvelous hotel does not suit, you can always try their luxurious spa for the day. "The Breakers Dining Collection" (as they have termed it) is impressive. From the **Seafood Bar**, to **Flagler Steakhouse**, to the elegant dinner dining in the **L'Escalier**, one of these dining delights should be on your agenda. Open only for breakfast, **The Circle Dining Room** is a favorite of mine, with its ocean views and magnificent hand painted ceiling. Although closed, this grand room's balcony (which during prohibition was home to the "private club") evokes memories and smiles. There is also a group of shops that should not be overlooked, especially **The Breakers News & Gourmet**, which not only has newspapers, magazines, books and culinary/dining accessories, but also coffees, pastries and a fine collection of the hotel's gourmet products. (Where else can one purchase Rose Petal Jelly?) Obtain a cup of coffee and a pastry and go and sit in the big white wicker chairs on the porch, or find a quiet place in the garden. For a nominal price, you will have enjoyed the fantastic ambiance of The Breakers.

The Henry Morrison Flagler Museum is the former home of Mr. and Mrs. Flagler and is a true treasure. Henry Flagler, who developed Palm Beach, built Whitehall for his bride, Mary Keenan. It is a step back in time to the Gilded Age.

The Palm Beach Historic Inn on South County Road is a charming place in the Historic Town Square District. As their brochure states: "Romance . . . Relax . . . Rejuvenate." That will be achieved easily at this delightful property, a bed and breakfast of special merit.

Green's Pharmacy on North County Road is popular among the locals, although I have yet to go there myself. Rumor has it that they serve very good diner-style meals.

The Church Mouse, the resale shop of the Bethesda-by-the-Sea Episcopal Church, is a treasure trove of the cast-offs of the well to do, featuring donated clothing, objets d'art, and various other items. Similarly, **The Goodwill Embassy Boutique** is not your typical Goodwill thrift shop. Some of the apparel at these shops look as if they have been worn a total of 15 minutes. For gifts, collectibles, and estate items visit **Tanya Pierce** at Via Vesta #3 in the middle of Sunset Avenue.

Do not leave the island without taking a drive up and down and all along **South County Road** and **Ocean Boulevard**. The houses—small castles, really—are definitely impressive and offer beautiful ocean views. Henry Flagler certainly knew a good thing when he decided to develop this little island.

MIAMI

Dazzling and dangerous, vibrant and eclectic, Miami can be intimidating to the solo female traveler. Because good and bad neighborhoods can be contiguous, it is important to have good directions and know where you are going at all times. I often leave the car behind and use taxis, especially when venturing out at night. **Bal Harbour**, the exclusive shopping enclave in North Miami, is a shoppers delight.

South Beach, famous for its art deco, pastel-colored hotels, is a people-watching treat. A typical past time is to sit on the patio of one of the beach side restaurants and observe all manner of humanity walk, roller blade, or sashay by. There are wonderful restaurants of all varieties, and interesting shops of all kinds. The area is relatively safe but one must, as always, be careful.

South of Miami, upscale **Coral Gables** has remained almost unchanged since the 1920s. It is worth a drive around to see the wide streets, fountains, plazas and if possible visit the grand **Biltmore Hotel**.

US 1 South actually starts in Van Buren, Maine and goes all the way to Key West, Florida. Going south from Miami it is not so much a scenic route, but rather one on which you will find some interesting shopping opportunities. **Designer Shoe Warehouse** can be found in the Kendall area on the north side of US 1. **The Falls**, an area full of the best stores and restaurants, is also just off US 1 and clearly marked by the imposing Bloomingdale's. Other unique places along US 1 that are among my favorites are **Cauley Square**, a historic site with a wonderful tea room and shops just off of the highway; **Monkey Jungle**; and just south of Homestead, **Coral Castle**. Coral Castle features a hand-carved coral home creation by Ed Leedskalnin. An amazing feat. Everything—from furniture to bathtubs—is made out of coral.

THE FLORIDA KEYS

It is in the Keys that US 1 is also called The Overseas Highway. There are two ways to figure out where you are in the Keys. The numbered addresses on US 1/ Overseas Highway, or by Mile Markers. MM 0 is Key West; MM 127 is Florida City.

Unique and beautiful are the Florida Keys. They were even more so before "civilization" arrived and deposited the trappings of modern living everywhere. The Keys are a string of various-sized islands that stretch south from the mainland at Homestead. The actual "keys" begin in Key Largo and continue on to Key West. They are connected by the unique Overseas Highway, built on the railroad tracks of the legendary Florida and East Coast Railroad. This railroad, built by Henry Flagler, linked the early resort areas of St. Augustine and Palm Beach with Miami and Key West, but was demolished by the hurricane of 1935. The state of Florida bought what remained of the railroad and constructed the Overseas Highway on top of it.

The more roundabout way to the Keys is via Card Sound Bridge. To do this you will turn off US 1 just south of Homestead and Florida City. Get in the left lane and watch carefully on US 1 for the overhead sign. If you miss this turn you will be on US 1 and there is no turning around until Key Largo. On Card Sound Road is **Alabama Jacks Restaurant**, an unusual roadside restaurant that people get to by whatever means possible: foot, car, boat, motorcycle, or bicycle. The place can be especially lively on the weekends, when live music is played.

There is a lot to do in the Keys. Arriving in Key Largo, you will get your first "feel" for the Keys at **The John Pennecamp Coral Reef State Park** and the **Maritime Museum of the Florida Keys**. An excellent restaurant is **The Sundowner** at MM103.9 (on the right side as you head south. You are not alone if you miss it the first time that you try to find it), a Keys landmark for food, drink and watching the sunset. It is best to make a reservation and arrive about 15 minutes before sun goes down. Another eatery, **The Fish House Restaurant and Market** at MM102.4 is casual and the food excellent. At the market you can buy a variety of fish to cook on your own, but it will be hard to beat what you eat at the restaurant. While not fancy, **Tower of Pizza** at MM100.5 provides decent Italian food. **Harriette's Restaurant**, 95710 Overseas Highway in Key Largo, is a wonderful, homey restaurant with equally wonderful homemade selections. For shopping, **Trade Winds Plaza** in Key Largo offers your basic Publix and K-Mart-type stores, but for the offbeat you will want to visit the **Pink Junktique** at MM98.2 on US 1 northbound. (US 1 is split by a commercial area here.) This shop is a treasure of vintage, contemporary, and unique consignments.

ISLAMORADA SOUTH TO KEY WEST

Considered by many the "Sportfishing Capital of the World," Islamorada is home to one of the more upscale hotels in the Keys, **Cheeca Lodge.** A delightful oasis with fine dining, a Friday-night seafood buffet is the staple year-round, with a Sunday buffet added in the winter (which of course is the high season). The Lodge is also in the process of adding a spa. South of Islamorada **Marathon** and **Pigeon Keys, Seven Mile Bridge, Bahia Honda State Park** and **Big Pine** are all worth stopping at to enjoy if only briefly. If time and money permit, you should plan a meal if not a night's stay at **Little Palm Island** off of **Little Torch Key,** the next Key after Big Pine and accessible only by boat. The facilities are so private that unless you are actually checked in to the hotel you can only go to the eating areas. Just before you get to Key West there is a wonderful, tiny restaurant called **Mango Mama's** at MM20. It is friendly and reasonably priced.

KEY WEST

Whatever unique, eclectic and eccentric places you have visited they will probably pale in comparison to Key West. Everything has been squeezed into Key West and no one seems to mind if anything runs over, wherever it runs over to! The streets are narrow, as are the sidewalks. There is some parking on the street or in designated lots. On your first visit it is advisable to take the Conch ("konk") Train/Tour and get a feel for the place and then go and explore whatever has tempted you from brochures or word of mouth. The **Hemingway House,** where the author wrote many of his most popular books, is worth a visit so long as you like cats. The place is full of them.

Do not leave the Keys without trying Yellowtail Snapper and Key Lime Pie.

GEORGIA

Georgia along I 95 is what I am most knowledgeable about, since I travel it on my way to Florida. Georgia is a surprisingly diversified state where both the New South and the Old South blend well. **Atlanta,** a big, bustling city, can be confusing to find your way around, so always get explicit directions. A better idea is to simply park your car and take a bus or a taxi. For the shopper, **Buckhead** is the place to go. Also worth seeing is **The Fox Theater**, a grand and ornate relic of the Depression era. **Macon** seems to be the place to go for antiquing; many wonderful shops. **Brunswick,** which is smack on I 95, is what I call a "Highway Hub" because of all the motels and fast food restaurants there. If you are traveling in peak tourist season and you plan to stop in Brunswick, I definitely recommend that you make a reservation. Note: There are few services between Brunswick and the Florida state line, so make sure you are well-provisioned before heading off.

Before we leave Georgia, I want to tell you about **The Cloister on Sea Island.** From reliable and honest sources, I quote and share this with you: "The Cloister is absolutely female friendly. It is huge and beautiful. There is little not to enjoy at this special spot." Perhaps by the time the next edition of this book appears I will have some first-hand information for you.

IDAHO
Coming into Idaho from the Jackson Hole area one can take spectacular **Teton Pass,** a true brake-burner of a road in places with some white-knuckle curves. Be sure to gas up in Wilson, just outside of Jackson on the Wyoming side. Needless to say it can be treacherous in winter, so an alternate route should be considered.

Victor and **Driggs,** Idaho, on the other side of the pass, are delightful, small towns. Victor is home to **Reel Women Fly Fishing Adventures.** (For more details see Wyoming.) From there into **Boise** roads in Idaho are generally good and the people friendly.

Arriving in Boise, I was surprised to find it so big. The area is beautiful. I visited the impressive University and also discovered that Boise is home of one of my very favorite grocery stores: Albertson's. A classmate whom I was visiting took me to the antique area. She lived in **Eagle**, which is an absolutely beautiful, bucolic area. The roads are slightly confusing (at least to this visitor), so again I suggest that you get detailed directions.

ILLINOIS
CHICAGO
Although difficult to get into at times by car due to heavy traffic, Chicago is a delight once you get there. It's best just to leave your car at the hotel and explore the city by its excellent public transportation system. It is a wonderful city in almost every way.

As for places to stay, the **Chicago Hilton and Towers** is a personal favorite. Originally the Stevens Hotel, it was at one time the largest hotel in the world. The Hilton, which will celebrate its 75th anniversary in 2002, is a small city in itself, yet the rooms are private, quiet, and very comfortable. There is always a lot going on at the Hilton; there can be a wedding reception in one ballroom and, at the same time, a full-blown convention downstairs in the basement meeting rooms. The hotel features four restaurants: casual dining at **The Pavilion** and **The Terrace**; more elegant fare at **Buckingham's**; and authentic Irish pub food at **Kitty O'Shea's**. **The Lakeside Green Lounge** is a very pleasant place to have a drink alone, and also doubles as a "grab and go" breakfast bar in the morning. The Hilton and Towers offers a broad range of rooms and suites; it's best to consult their website at *www.chicago-hilton.com* to find the best rate and any special promotions.

Two other fine hotels are **The Drake**, with its dignity, sophistication and old world charm, and **The Palmer House** (also part of the Hilton chain), definitely a Chicago landmark.

Buses in Chicago are a great way to get around and fares can be paid with dollar bills. I found the bus drivers to be extremely helpful and friendly—some even sharing jokes to enliven your ride. Everybody in Chicago seems to be helpful, friendly and fun. Of course the city is perhaps best known for its magnificent architecture and fine museums, so I would recommend taking advantage of the many tours that are available.

Chicago is a shopper's Valhalla. **The Magnificent Mile** on North Michigan Avenue is full of delights, from Neiman Marcus to the corner drug store. **State Street** still echoes of "that great street," and contains two of the remaining old world major department stores, **Marshall Field** and **Carson Pirie Scott & Co**. One of my great shopping "finds" in Chicago, however, was not a department store but **Hidden Treasures**, a specialty retail shop at 46 East Chicago Avenue that supports hospital programs.

Leaving Chicago is almost as difficult as entering it. Before venturing out be sure to double check the directions as to how to get to the highway you want. From downtown to the interstate there are pockets of areas where a woman would feel uncomfortable having to ask directions. I did get terribly lost once, but thanks to a friendly police officer whose first name was "Champagne," I was able to pop out of the city like a cork leaving a bottle.

Interstate 64W is easy and the large farms that you pass are absolutely beautiful. You cross the Ohio River outside Louisville and for a very short time you are in Indiana. Then you cross the Wabash River and you are in Illinois for a short time. It was around Mt. Vernon, Illinois that I stopped for gas and discovered **Dobbs**, a unique department store. It is a very large building with everything from the cheap items to the necessities, the latter seeming to me a bit expensive.

INDIANA

OK, so I've only just passed through Indiana, traveling from Louisville to St. Louis on I 64. I can tell you that the road was good and the scenery most pleasant.

IOWA

I 80 west from Chicago was a little rough the last time I drove it—but perhaps the road has been repaired by now. From the state line to Des Moines there are plenty of places to stop for a night, but I favor **The Hampton Inn** in Davenport because, you guessed it, there are places in the area to go shopping.

Walcott, Iowa boasts the world's largest truck stop, **Iowa 80**, a Truckstops of America franchise, where you are greeted with the sign **Chapel Dentist Massage**. What a combo! When I stopped there I was not in need of any of these services, but the whole operation prompted me to search out the marketing director, who provided me with the following Iowa 80 fun facts: In the 36 years of being in business 12,500,000 eggs have been served; 1.5 million cups of coffee are served per year; and over 55 million customers have been served. The store contains 50,000 items, and the truck stop sees 5,000 customers a day. There is also a 300-seat restaurant with a 50-foot-long salad bar and several fast food options, and the list of "amenities" goes on. Although this "stop" is crowded I feel a woman can feel safe here—and actually at all Truck Stops of America.

From what I hear, you just might want to plan your trip around the **Walcott Truckers Jamboree** that is held in July. I guarantee your memories will be priceless. You will be able to recall the Super Truck Beauty Contest, eating 1½ inch-thick Iowa Pork Chops, enjoying live music, and viewing 100 Antique Trucks. Who could ask for more?

East of 80 there are plenty of places to stop for "food, gas, and lodging," but **Williamsburg** and **Grinnell** probably have the most to offer, especially at Williamsburg, where there is a large outlet mall.

I 80 West will take you to Des Moines and then on to Omaha via US 680 and I 29 south. Or you can take I 80 to Council Bluffs and then follow signs for Omaha.

KENTUCKY
The interstates in Kentucky are generally very good, but remember to keep track of identification markers, since there are long stretches of the interstate without much around. The roads around Lexington can be a bit confusing as several come together like spokes to a hub. Make sure you know where you are going.

HARRODSBURG
An absolutely delightful place to visit and spend the night is **The Beaumont Inn** in Harrodsburg. Here you are in the heart of Bluegrass Country and you will pass some of the most famous racing stables in the country –if not in the world—on your way to the Inn. The Beaumont Inn was originally built as a girl's school and became an Inn around 1880. It has been run by the same family for four generations. The Victorian décor blends with an abundant mix of antiques to provide the perfect setting to enjoy their absolutely delicious Southern cuisine, such as Country Ham, corn pudding and General Robert E. Lee Orange-lemon Cake. There is nothing pretentious about this property; the people are easy-going and the whole experience like a step back in time, from the soft peal of the dinner bell to the "Beaumont cocktail"—a glass of ice water placed by your bed at night.

LOUISVILLE
The Brown Hotel, located in downtown, is a 4 Diamond 4 Star property with 293 attractively appointed rooms. The service is

excellent, including such amenities as a complementary shoeshine and a hot water bottle placed in your bed at turn-down (if you wish it). **The Brown Antique Shop** is among the many exquisite shops on the property. Whether you are staying at the hotel or just popping your head in, do not miss enjoying a Hot Brown sandwich in the restaurant. Two beautiful theaters, **The Brown** and **The Palace**, are just down the block from the hotel and are worth seeing. Another famous historic Louisville hotel is **The Seelbach**, just down the street from The Brown. Although I have only walked around the lobby and a few of the other public rooms, from what I have seen it is beautiful. A fabulous example of Victorian Romanesque Revival architecture is **The Conrad/Caldwell House**, which is open to the public and is located just a short distance from The Brown Hotel in what was one of the first residential areas of Louisville.

Although I did not have a chance to visit them, **The Derby Museum** and **Grapevine Pantry** (excellent soups, chicken salad, and meringue pies, or so I hear) have been highly recommended by a lady friend for my next trip to Louisville.

MAINE

Traveling in Maine is a delight. It is a huge state, and I 95 will take you from the bottom to almost the top of the state. It's a good road, although the traffic at the lower part of the state tends to be congested. I 95 will take you to Portland and north to **Freeport**, home of **LL Bean**. Don't worry about getting to the store before it closes, for it is open 24 hours a day, 365 days a year. From Freeport you can stay on I 95 to Bangor and on to the Canadian border, but far more interesting is to take US 1 at Brunswick, which goes straight up the Maine coast. Try not to be in a rush because there are so many charming places to stop at and visit, see, eat, buy, browse and chat. **Camden** is a quaint but sophisticated town that has definitely been "discovered," so it might not be quaint for very long. I stayed at **The Whitehall Inn** and enjoyed its nostalgic charms. Reservations are suggested, even if you are just having dinner at The Whitehall.

The towns of Belfast, Searsport, Bucksport, Ellsworth are all on US 1. In **Searsport** I saw a small sign that enticed me—I really do not remember what it said, but I drove into the driveway, got out of the car and walked into an open garage. What treasures I found! There on about eight long tables were boxes with title cards categorizing topics of articles from magazines, newspapers, etc. As I found out later from the owner and organizer of all this, **Sandra Baker**, she calls her business "Visual Images and Articles on Any Subject." I found many pieces I wanted to take home and frame, but I had to exercise some self-control. But what a find!

East off of US 1 are Blue Hill, Southwest Harbor, Northeast Harbor, Bar Harbor, and Acadia National Park. In between these towns can be found some adorable treasures, which may be worth looking into since many of the more populated places can be pricey in the high season. **Northeast Harbor** is quietly sophisticated, somewhat elite, charming and posh, but in its own way, homey. **The Asticou Inn** is definitely a place to stay or at least go visit. **The Maison Suisse Inn** is small, charming and ever so cozy. Located downtown on Main Street, it is within easy walking distance of many wonderful shops, including the intriguing **Romantic Room**, which has a colorful and eclectic mix of items for every room and for you.

Acadia National Park is truly beautiful and not to be missed. A $10.00 pass allows you to come and go for a week. Be sure to take the 27-mile Park Loop. If your polar bear genes surface you can go for a swim in the beautiful waters. **Bar Harbor** is worth a visit if you can put up with crowds and tourist traps.

Several cruises ranging in length from one to three hours on the **Sea Princess** are available and highly recommended. These cruises are in calm, wonderful waters and I have never had a bad time on any of them. If you have time for only one cruise, I vote for the one to Cranberry Island.

If, during your Maine drives, you pass a farm and you see cows in the field that look like no other cow you have ever seen, do not think you have lost it. What you are looking at are Belted Galloways, black or brown cows that have a broad white band circling their midriffs (if that is what you call the middle part of a cow).

MARYLAND
From the south well-patrolled US 13 enters Maryland and proceeds to Salisbury, a hub of highways that offers a number of

attractive options. Staying on US 13 will put you in Delaware; US 50 west will take you to the beautiful areas of Cambridge, Oxford, St. Michaels, and Easton on the Chesapeake Bay, and then north to the Chesapeake Bay Bridge (not to be confused with the Chesapeake Bay Bridge Tunnel) and into Annapolis. (The Chesapeake Bay Bridge is a bit creepy for this driver—the side rails are open and the road surface is like a steel grate. You feel like you are going to go into the water.)

US 50 east of Salisbury takes you to popular **Ocean City**, which can be a zoo on weekends in summer.

Annapolis is a charming mix of a town with seaport amenities, crooked little streets, a potpourri of historic buildings, and of course the **US Naval Academy**. Another way to get to Annapolis is via US 301, which starts in Delaware. The northern part of this road is quite bucolic, and then it becomes more congested by Waldorf, White Plains, and La Plata. But there are a lot of shopping places and sizeable malls in this area.

Baltimore, once a "gritty city," has given itself a facelift in recent years and is worth a visit, especially to the **Inner Harbor**, where you can tour the U.S. Frigate *Constellation* and visit the wonderful **National Aquarium**.

MICHIGAN
Michigan is a big, beautiful state with good roads, but that's what you would expect from the state that is home to "Motor City."

DETROIT
Detroit is experiencing a much-needed renaissance on every level, but still, women traveling alone should be very careful. Be sure to have good directions to your destination, since roads and streets are not particularly well marked and it is easy to get in a neighborhood that is not safe. However, places such as **Greektown** are worth visiting for their fine ethnic foods and ambiance. I stayed at the **Atheneum Suite** Hotel right in the heart of Greektown where I felt safe and comfortable. My room, called the Premium Suite, was spacious and contained an un-enclosed jacuzzi that overlooked the sunken bedroom.(That was a first!) **Fishbone's** is a popular restaurant that connects directly to the hotel.

DEARBORN

Dearborn is a pleasant city and boasts the world headquarters of the **Ford Motor Company**. Of particular interest is **The Henry Ford Estate**, a short, easy drive from the **Hyatt** downtown, where I was staying. The Hyatt is a friendly hotel and one that welcomes women and is most aware of safety concerns. Parking is on the property in the adjacent lot. The **Ford Museum** is impressive and one should not rush through it, but allow a few hours to enjoy the inside and out. The gardens are beautiful. Across from the Hyatt is the **Fairlane Town Center**, a very nice shopping complex. There are lots of favorite places here, but at the top of the list is **Off Fifth**, the outlet for discounted Saks Fifth Avenue's merchandise.

GRAND RAPIDS

Grand Rapids is an easy drive from Chicago via I 94 to Benton Harbor. You will be following the Lake Michigan coastline through some absolutely picturesque small towns with quaint stores and attractive antique shops. In spring and summer flowers are bright and abundant. People are friendly and everything is very clean. At Benton Harbor I 96 leaves the coast and takes you directly into Grand Rapids.

Grand Rapids is, to me anyway, a surprisingly big city. The roads are well marked and converge on downtown. A convenient place to stay is the **Amway Grand Plaza Hotel**; though large (over 600 rooms) it is attractive and friendly with much to keep one occupied: shopping, admiring the collections of art, or just deciding which of the eight restaurants to try.

MACKINAW CITY & MACKINAC ISLAND

From the "west coast" of Michigan I 196 takes you north to where you can cut over to I 75 and proceed directly to Mackinaw City. In Mackinaw City, you leave your car and board the ferry to Mackinac Island, where cars are not permitted. The twenty-minute ferry boat ride to the island costs about $15.00 and is worth every penny. The scenery is beautiful.

Few places are as unique, beautiful, romantic, and spellbinding as **Grand Hotel** (Incidentally, "The" does not precede "Grand Hotel"). This huge white structure features rocking chairs that line an enormous porch, bright red geraniums, bellowing American flags, carriages, and the clomping sounds of horses' hooves. This is a most special place; the movie *Some-where in Time* was filmed here. Even if you cannot spend a night at Grand Hotel you can enjoy a tour for a minimum charge, or indulge in Afternoon Tea, which is presented and served to perfection. If you can spend the night, be ready to dress-up for dinner, a tradition that has survived our lapse into informality. If you are dining alone, I recommend a window table, where you can watch people strolling on the porch or just become enthralled by the scenery. The dining staff is most attentive. Also under the aegis of the hotel is **Woods**, a wonderful restaurant that was originally part of the **Stonecliffe Mansion**. Regardless of your length of stay, you will be forever glad to have visited Grand Hotel and Mackinac Island.

Mackinac Island itself is a bit touristy, but the charm of the place can overcome that. There is a lot of fascinating history, so I'd recommend obtaining a map, stepping into some sturdy, comfortable walking shoes and giving yourself a tour. Although the terrain is not totally flat it is not in any way difficult. You can also rent a bicycle and tour the island that way.

Once back on the mainland and in your car you may wish to take I 75 south toward Flint, and if so I highly recommend a stop at **Birch Run Prime Outlets**, exit 136. I 75 itself is a great highway and very scenic. There are billboards announcing attractions for the avid hunter and yes, a "Federal Facility" sign reminding you not to pick up hitchhikers. There are stretches that do not have any facilities, so be sure to keep gas tank at least half full.

MINNESOTA
Minnesota, a big state known for its cold weather and eccentric governor, Jesse Ventura, is a beautiful place to visit in the summer. Of particular interest to me was the Mississippi Valley; simply watching boats navigate the locks was fascinating, and it is scenic as well.

WABASHA
Wabasha is straight up the Mississippi on US 61 from I 95, past the town of Winona (where there is a Target store and a gas station, if you need them). When I arrived in Wabasha I

felt like I had stumbled across a movie set. This is where *Grumpy Old Men* was written. Wabasha is spotless, and the countryside river-beautiful. In Wabasha you feel as if you are actually stepping into a different era with its relaxed, wonderful lifestyle. It has a mix of interesting shops, and many of the original structures are being restored or just remaining "as is" until needed. The river seems to be the center of activity, from fishing to bald eagle watching; the **Delta Queen** and other river cruise ships call at Wabasha as well.

Another way of stepping back in time is to visit the landmark hotel, **Anderson House**, on West Main Street. In addition to the usual amenities, Anderson House can offer you a cat to keep you company. Apparently, back in 1896 Grandmother Anderson had lots of cats at her hotel, and when she passed away and her heirs took over the cats remained. Now some of the cats' descendants are in residence. When you check into Anderson House you are asked if you would like a cat in your room during your stay. No extra charge, of course, for a cat companion. You can go to the cat suite and pick one of the fifteen resident cats to warm your feet or perhaps use as a sounding board for your thoughts. Perhaps a cat is not your desire or need, but there is an alternative: you can get a mustard plaster or a hot brick in a quilted envelope. The food at Anderson House is authentic, true home cooking and is delicious. You will not find nouvelle cuisine with confetti outlining the food and circling the rim of your plate, because there is simply no room on the plate for trendy decorations. Be sure to try the famous sticky buns and always save room for dessert.

The rates at Anderson House are reasonable, and children are welcome. There are special packages for the man or woman traveling alone.

Behind the hotel there is an ice cream shop, and here I found myself one Fourth of July on the porch with several of the other guests, all of us sitting in rocking chairs watching the fireworks. Norman Rockwell could not have painted a more American scene.

The **L.A.R.K Toy Factory** is a very short drive from Wabasha and is a great place to do some Christmas shopping, whatever time of year it is. There you will see and can ride their new carousel with 20 hand-carved animals. There are restaurants, toy museums and a lot to see and to be tempted to buy. It will bring out the child within you.

MISSOURI
ST. LOUIS

St. Louis is a true "hub" city where several major interstates (70, 55, 44, 64) meet. I was surprised to discover how many other major cities in nearby states are truly just a stone's throw from St. Louis.

For my visit to St. Louis I had the hotel fax me specific directions, which is something everyone should consider when venturing into a city for the first time. The directions were excellent. The hotel itself, **The Hyatt Regency at Union Station**, is built around St. Louis's old rail station; the lobby of the hotel is the famed Union Station Grand Hall, built in 1894 and once deemed the largest and most beautiful terminal in the United States. It has been completely restored, from its barrel-vaulted ceiling with Romanesque arches, to the stained glass windows and ornate moldings. So much happened at this station that a self-guided walking tour will bring much of this magnificent structure's history alive. (Discover the secret of The "Whispering Arch.") Also on site are restaurants, specialty shops, marketplaces, stores, and (unbelievably) a one-acre lake.

Do not leave St. Louis without visiting the **Gateway Arch** on the St. Louis riverfront. To learn how it was constructed is fascinating. In order to get to the top of the arch, one must ride in a small 4-seat "compartment," an experience that is not for the claustrophobic. There is also a museum and several displays pertaining to westward expansion.

MONTANA

The largest of the Rocky Mountain states, Montana is truly beautiful, from Glacier National Park in the north to Yellowstone in the south. I did not find a thing in Montana that could be considered unpleasant for a woman.

GARDINER

Just over the state line, about five miles from Mammoth Hot Springs in Yellowstone, is the tiny, hippie town of Gardiner, population 852. Rustic, low key, but with hints of real savviness, this is one of those places where you will definitely feel welcome. I enjoyed a meal at the **Loft Restaurant**, which is on the second floor of the **Town Café and Motel**. After dinner I explored town and discovered the **Yankee Jim Trading Post**, **Gardiner Drug Store**, and **Wood N' Stitches Embroidery Shop**. Thank goodness I had not had dessert because in the Embroidery Shop is a bona fide, working soda fountain that has all sorts of delicious ice creams, as well as an egg cream for $1.50.

From Gardiner I ventured north toward Glacier National Park, where my younger son was working for the summer. Between Bozeman and Butte, there is a must-stop eatery in **The Oven Fresh Bakery and Deli** in **Three Forks**. To say that everything is absolutely delicious is a complete understatement, at least from my experience. The grains for the breads are freshly ground and the breads are continually being made. You cannot get bread any fresher. It is a popular spot and it can be crowded, but it is absolutely worth the wait (which didn't seem too long).

GLACIER NATIONAL PARK

Spectacular Glacier National Park contains several great hotels; I stayed at **The Many Glacier Hotel**, a rustic, friendly place that was completed in 1915. The staff puts on a weekly variety show here and even entertains in the dining rooms with musical selections.

There is so much to see and do in Glacier that it would be a good idea to plan your itinerary with professionals or get suggestions from those who have been to Glacier. Yes, you will see bears, probably lots of bears, but also bighorn sheep and other wildlife. Remember that you are on their turf and that they do not care to be disturbed—and you do not want them to disturb you.

One of the most magnificent experiences you can have in Glacier is driving **Going-to-the Sun Road**. The road twists and turns for 50 miles, giving you breathtaking views at each turn. You will go along the Garden Wall, cross the Continental Divide at Logan Pass (6,646 feet) and descend to St. Mary's Lake. There is no question that this road is a true engineering feat. Buses are available if you'd rather look than navigate the switchbacks for 50 miles. In St. Mary's there is the colorful **Two Sisters Café**, which I thoroughly enjoyed.

Leaving Glacier I picked up I 15 at Shelby then headed south to Great Falls, where I got on US 87 south (I was headed for Casper, Wyoming that night, a long haul). After getting gas in Lewiston I came upon **Grassrange**, where a country store loomed temptingly. What a delight this turned out to be! The "store" part of the establishment is on one side, overseen by men. The restaurant part is on the other side and that, of course, is run by women. When I arrived the homemade sweet buns were just coming out of the oven. Wow! It was a wonderful stop.

NEBRASKA
OMAHA
A delightful surprise, Omaha is a pocket full of treasures. The **Sheraton Omaha** in historic downtown is a place a woman can feel secure in. The hotel self-parking is convenient and safe. The property itself is attractive and well run and within walking distance of the Old Market district. Cobblestone streets and nineteenth-century buildings are now filled with boutiques, bookstores, restaurants and whatever is trendy.

NEVADA
WENDOVER WEST (WENDOVER, UTAH)
Obviously these two towns are on the border and Wendover West, being the first city in Nevada along I 80, is a big gambling town. Even so, women can feel secure, although this is not Mayberry by any means. It is important to be alert, look like you know what you are doing (even if you don't), and know where you are going. Drinks are often free in the casinos, but don't be too tempted.

The State Line Hotel proved to be comfortable and friendly in spite of its size (800+ rooms) and it is clean. There are a lot of other hotels and motels, as well as the usual fast-food establishments and, of course, pawnshops. Pawnshops come in several varieties: very professional establishments, rough shops that are willing to take your blood if that is all you have to offer, and friendly ones that are fun to look around in and maybe find a treasure or two.

The drive from Wendover West to Reno is quite long and will take you at least 8-9 hours, but it should be done at least once. Although the highway is excellent, I would not recommend driving I 80 across Nevada at night. There are long, desolate stretches and if you need help (heaven forbid) it could be a real problem. A cell phone is imperative. The road is dusty, windy, and full of trucks; the topography barren, flat, and at times monotonous—but it does have an aura that you should experience.

ELKO
This is the first *real* town you will come to. It has over 14,000 people and all the usual retail chain stores. I even found one of my favorites: Maurices. Elko would be a good place to stay overnight if you wanted to divide the trek across the state. It is a beautiful area for wildlife and outdoor sports.

RENO
With a population of over 133,000, Reno will look like a metropolis after Elko. It's a busy and crowded place, too, full of casinos, pawnshops, and all the riff-raff they attract. Although there are many hotels, I played it safe and stayed at the **Hilton**.

LAKE TAHOE
The drive into Tahoe from Reno on US 395 can be a slight brake burner, but it is not too bad. People are generally patient with those who drive slower than the natives, but look out for passing cars.

Tahoe is now very "in" for the Silicon Valley new money barons, and price seems not to be much of an object. It's a stunningly beautiful area, so it's no wonder.

Lake Tahoe is huge and straddles both Nevada and California. **Incline Village** is the Nevada area of Tahoe. **The Hyatt Regency, Lake Tahoe Resort & Casino** is a wonderful place to stay with its lakeside beach and mountain backdrop. When I was there the beach attendant was most considerate in reminding bathers of the intense sun at that altitude (6,000') and to apply sunscreen accordingly. Nearby are plenty of restaurants, a very nice grocery store, and a post office.

If you are heading west out of Tahoe and into California, be sure to top off the gas tank. There are not a lot of gas stations along this section of I 80.

LAS VEGAS

I 15 will take you to the ultimate of neon cities, the gambling and show town of Las Vegas. Whatever you have read or seen about Las Vegas will pale in comparison to seeing it first-hand. Because of the crowds, the money changing hands, the shows, and everything else that happens in Las Vegas, it is actually a relatively safe place for a woman to visit on her own. Police, security guards, and video cameras are every-where.

It has also become something of a destination for families, as well; there are plenty of things for children to do. It's best to plan well ahead of time for a stay in Las Vegas; many hotels sell out for the weekends, for example, and tickets to popular shows disappear quickly.

One travel tip I was told: If you're headed to Los Angeles, avoid leaving Las Vegas on a Sunday afternoon. It's a parking lot all the way to the coast.

NEW MEXICO

The interstates in New Mexico to and from Santa Fe are gen-erally good and well marked, but there are also long stretches of highway without many services. Be prepared, especially in winter.

SANTA FE

Santa Fe is growing rapidly, but its historic downtown re-mains its hub. Getting there is a little confusing as some streets are one way, usually away from the destination you are trying to get to.

Charming in many different ways, Santa Fe mixes old world with the tourist world—but that's fine. A map is advised for a self-guided walking tour. The Plaza with its inviting park is the center of the downtown historic area, and at the Palace of the Governors (at the Plaza) Native Americans arrive each morning to sell their wares. The shopping in Santa Fe is "world class."

You can see more on foot in Santa Fe than in many other cities; the museums, art galleries, and shops are all right there. There are also several major hotels within walking dis-tance of downtown. For dining, I recommend **The Plaza Restaurant**, a 50-year-old landmark. More like an over-sized diner, there are booths and tables as well as a long counter, an ideal place to eat and talk if one is alone. The food is good, the staff has never met a stranger and the price is right. **Hotel Loretto** in historic downtown is comfortable and very tastefully appointed. There are lots of shops within the hotel as well as a restaurant, which has a most friendly atmosphere. Next door is the **Loretto Chapel** with its remarkable twenty-two-foot high stairway, which has no center support. Constructed with wooden pegs, it has thirty-three steps and makes two complete 360-degree turns.

A charming oasis, **La Posada de Santa Fe Resort and Spa** is but a short walk from downtown. When you check in, you are handed a refreshing drink—a very nice touch. La Posada's ambiance is exceptional. A nice La Posada tradition (at least when I was there) is the afternoon wine and hors d'oeuvres that are served, gratis, in the library. It is a pleasant way to meet other guests. The award-winning **Inn of the Anasazi** and **Anasazi Restaurant** are a treasure and a delight. This small boutique hotel contains but fifty-nine southwestern-style, beautifully appointed, comfortable rooms that are truly luxurious. It is on a side street, Washington Avenue, just a short distance from the Palace of the Governors and the hub of old Santa Fe. Convenient valet parking is available. **La Fonda** is in downtown and a hub in itself with its many shops and attractions. The original adobe hotel was known to be "at the end of the Santa Fe Trail" where the trail ended at the town's plaza.

The Bishop's Lodge, a ranch resort for the entire family, is five minutes from downtown Santa Fe. Accommodations are attractive and the hospitality and food are friendly and delicious. There are all sorts of activities, including dance lessons! Be sure to get your copy of "Smoke Signals from the Concierge Desk," which will tell of happenings both at The Bishop's Lodge as well as in Santa Fe. There is a complementary year-round shuttle to town, and in the winter transportation to the nearby ski area.

Shopping is all too easy in Santa Fe. Remember to ask yourself, as you get caught-up in the frenzy, "Will I like this when I get back home?" If you just want to go for it, start with **Act 2: Vintage to Modern Clothing and Collectibles**, around the block from La Posada. A little too far to walk but a short drive is another shopping "must," **Encore 505: A Consignment Shop**. Fashionable, extremely well run and enjoyable, here I found some of my trademarks: great scarves! If you're in the mood for knickknacks, **Jackalope** is the place; you will have to drive, but it is not far, nor is it difficult to find as it is on one of the major thoroughfares. Santa Fe also has its fair share of retail chain stores such as **K–Mart**, **Ross** and **TJ Maxx**, handy for returning anything you might have bought at another one of their kindred stores in your travels.

A short drive from downtown Santa Fe on Old Taos Hwy is **Gabriel's**, home of some of the best ribs I've eaten. The guacamole and Caesar salad are prepared at your table, and the margaritas are made with premium tequila. The atmosphere is very casual but the food is very excellent. If you're by yourself, you can sit at the bar and have dinner and partake in friendly banter with your neighbors. This is a popular place so reservations are important.

Other activities in the Santa Fe area include its famous **Opera** (seasonal), the weekend **Flea Market**, the **Farmer's Market**, the **Spanish Market**, and the **Georgia O'Keeffe Museum**.

OJO CALIENTE
About an hour and fifteen minutes from downtown Santa Fe is Ojo Caliente, a hot springs oasis that contains seven different pools: iron, soda, mineral, arsenic, mud and two cliffside pools that are mixtures of all the waters. "Drinking any of the waters while bathing helps to eliminate excessive acids and other impurities, creating more vitality and energy," or so you are informed in the brochure. You can also obtain therapeutic massages and special body and facial treatments here. There are also mountain bike trails and horseback trails.

There is limited lodging but do try to spend the night. You will find it modest, but absolutely relaxing, probably because you've been soaking in a hot spring all day. Your room will consist of a clean bed, shag carpet, sink, clean towels and a toilet. However, as the brochure says: "Showers and tubs are not available in any of the rooms, as all bathing is done in the bath houses." There is no TV and no phone. There is a dining room, **The Artesian Restaurant** where (when I was there) the food and service rated many culinary stars. The experience at Ojo Caliente is delightfully unique and wonderful.

Other New Mexico places that are high on my list are **Rancho de San Juan,** a most gracious, quiet country inn and restaurant surrounded by the awesome Jemez Mountains, and **The Lodge at Chama,** possibly one of the most "upscale" hunting and fishing lodges I've ever been to.

NOTE: From Santa Fe the roads are excellent heading east to Texas. Be sure to take US 285, a superb road, to Clines Corners; this is a well-known "stop" where you will find all sorts of things. From Clines Corners you get directly on I 40, which will take you to Santa Rosa, Tucumcari and into Texas.

NEW YORK
NEW YORK CITY
Driving into New York City can be a bit of a challenge. Try not to do so at rush hour. If you are entering from the New Jersey Turnpike, be alert as drivers are fearless and are constantly jockeying for position. Do not let the honking of horns, hand gestures or facial expressions distract you. The tunnels into New York (Lincoln is midtown and Holland is downtown) both have tolls. As of this writing they were about $5.

Driving in and around the city your head must be on a swivel at all times. Be alert, fearless, and don't get upset with road rudeness. Today's NYC taxi drivers think they own the streets and drive accordingly. When I was a bit younger, a parent could put her daughter in a taxi cab and let her go to her friend's house, or to dancing school, and feel perfectly secure. When I was older, I remember talking to a taxi driver as if he was my personal psychologist. You'd get to your destination, the meter would stop, you'd pay the fare and you'd get out of the cab feeling better for a therapeutic conversation with someone you'd never see again. Oh those worldly taxi drivers. So much for memories. Regardless of where you are in the city, drivers consider an inch between cars to be a safe driving distance. This driving disease is contagious. Stay immune.

Parking in New York is a hassle. If you park on the street be aware that the parking rules are strictly enforced. Street parking works if you park in a "sensible" area and the parking rules happen to fit your schedule. Do not leave things in your car that are important, and never leave items exposed. Garage parking is expensive, more so in busy and popular areas. Garage stories are rampant, but use your street sense when choosing a garage. If you have a friend in the city get his or her advice. Many hotels have garages or are affiliated with one, but this will cost you as well. You might just give some consideration to leaving your car at a suburban rail station and taking the train into town.

New York has everything you could possibly want and then a bit that you might not want. New York is well laid out and not difficult to find your way around, once you know the order of the streets and avenues. And, notwithstanding the tragic events of September 11, 2001, it is still the greatest city in the world. Though "Ground Hero" remains a mass grave for fallen Americans as of this writing, it may help you deal with the crisis to pay your respects to the firemen, police, and ordinary citizens who lost their lives to the dark forces in the world. But as Mayor Guliani has said, the best thing you can do to help New York and New Yorkers is to come to the city and spend a little money.

New York is a great walking city if you are so inclined, but the buses and subways are easy and a bargain. However, you must have exact change for the bus, and coins, not dollar bills. You can get a subway/bus card at almost any grocery store, subway station, etc. The cards, which can be day passes, week passes, whatever, will eliminate the need for you to carry ten pounds of quarters around with you.

When one says New York City, certain sights immediately come to mind: **The Empire State Building; Macy's; Central Park** with its zoo and merry go round; **Park Avenue, Fifth Avenue**, and **Wall Street**; the **United Nations**, and then the most distinguished and elegant **Waldorf-Astoria**. Occupying an entire city block on Park Avenue from 49th to 50th Streets and over to Lexington Avenue, the building defies description. One only has to walk from the Park Avenue entrance through the famous lobby and out the Lexington Avenue side to realize why it has achieved only superlatives. Be sure to walk slowly, enjoy the art and possibly sit in the lobby near the famous clock and watch the scene. You will not be disappointed. Please dress nicely because the Grand Dame deserves a lot of respect. Dining at one of the restaurants will be memorable. Be sure to try the famous rice pudding!

There are a zillion restaurants in NYC but I mention Tavern On The Green, in Central Park, because it has convenient parking and is an outstanding restaurant.

Shopping

On Third Avenue between 85th and 79th Streets there are several wonderful thrift shops. **Cancer Care** on Third and 85th has lots of treasures and a friendly staff. There are also other thrift shops. **The Spence Chapin Thrift Shop** is in two locations, but my favorite is on Second Avenue and 95th. The other in on Third and about 84th. The **NCJW Thrift Shop** is between Second and Third on 84th Street. These are all fun and fabulous haunts.

If you want to have a luxurious vicarious thrill, then the 57th Street area on Fifth Avenue is where you go. Here you will find **Tiffany's**, a four-story jewel box, and **Bergdorf Goodman**, a simply beautiful store. I take the elevator to the 7th floor to use the spacious and clean ladies room, directly to your left as you get off the elevator. The view from the ladies room window overlooks Central Park and you can see forever (if the air is clear). Bergdorf's 7th floor is gift wares, antiques, old hotel ware, books, and stationery. If this is not enough for you, then you can venture out on to 57th Street and visit the boutiques and upscale stores between Sixth and Third Avenues. For the early riser, **The CBS Early Show** can be taken in at nearby Trump Plaza (Fifth Avenue and 59th Street). **FAO Schwartz** is right there for the child in you. Across the street is the famed **Plaza Hotel**, definitely worth a walk-through and possibly a sit-down for tea in the Palm Court or a drink in the Oak Room.

Further down on Fifth Avenue is **Rockefeller Plaza,** a city unto itself. Take a tour if possible. If you go in the 30 Rockefeller Entrance, be sure to look up at the ceiling mural of Atlas, specifically at his head as you walk from one side to the other. Rockefeller Plaza is also where you can watch **The Today Show** through heavy, plate glass windows, and enjoy one of the fabulous Today Show outdoor concerts in season.

Broadway is chaotic, colorful, contagious, corrupting. It is walkable from 57th Street, but a sensible alternative is a bus. On 44th and Broadway at Times Square are the new studios of ABC's **Good Morning America**. To be part of the "inside audience" you have to call the network, but if you want to be part of the "outside audience" then just get up early and arrive. **The Stage Delicatessen** and **The Ed Sullivan Theater** should be on your list to visit as well. You had best be hungry at The Stage. Think of splitting a sandwich with someone as they are huge, and then you will possibly have room for dessert. The Ed Sullivan Theater is home to *The David Letterman Show,* for which tickets are required if you decide to go. I have a very special feeling for this place since it was here that I was a Production Assistant for Kodak, on the Ed Sullivan Show when live TV was really live and wonderfully unpredictable.

A more sedate way to see the city would be to take a tour bus and/or the **Circle Line** around Manhattan. Ferries also go out to the Statue of Liberty and Ellis Island, but it is advisable to get an early start to avoid long lines.

NYC is full of treasures, not the least of which are the exceptional museums: **The Metropolitan, The Museum of Modern Art, The Whitney, The Cooper Hewitt, The Museum of the City of New York,** and **The Museum of Television and Radio.**

The highways in and out of New York City are quite well marked, but be aware that sometimes the same road will have two different names. **The Taconic Parkway** is beautiful but full of curves, and in winter it can be tricky as ice patches form quickly.

LONG ISLAND
There is no question that Long Island is no longer the quiet area of farmed fields, duck farms, and quaint villages with the ocean just a stone's throw away. Getting there from New York City can be a hassle as well, especially on a summer weekend. There are a few precious enclaves, such as the Hamptons, that are worth visiting, but don't expect to save any money there.

NORTH CAROLINA
I 95 is what I travel the most through North Carolina, and my favorite stopping place is the **Carolina Outlet Center** in Smithfield. There are about 80 brand name stores to indulge yourself in, including **Carolina Pottery, The Fashion Outlet** and **Harry and David's,** where I usually pick a snack to eat in the car. You can definitely make a full day of this outlet center, but limit your time if you are driving on.

ASHEVILLE
Sophisticated, hip, and interesting, Asheville boasts many attractive shops, great places to eat, and wonderful places to

stay. The approach into Asheville on I 40 over **Black Mountain** is breathtaking, especially in the fall, but remember to keep your eyes on the road. With its well-marked roadways Asheville is easy to explore, and parking is not difficult downtown. There are numerous places to eat, but a personal favorite of mine is the **Blue Moon Bakery** downtown.

The historic **Grove Park Inn Resort and Spa**, built with giant boulders and stone and oak woodwork, is famous for its arts and crafts furnishings and beautiful setting. The mammoth fireplace in the baronial main hall is as big as some studio apartment kitchens. You can dine on the Sunset Terrace and take in the breathtaking view of the countryside. **The Gingerbread House Contest**, usually around the middle of November, is not to be missed. The spa opened in 2001 to rave reviews. It is a 40,000 square-foot subterranean facility that is called by some the finest spa in North America. In downtown, the **Haywood Park Hotel** is a small, delightful property, unique because it was originally a department store. There are tempting shops and the hotel is convenient to all of downtown.

The famed **Biltmore Estate** is a short drive from Asheville, but worth every turn of your tires to see how the other half once lived. This 250-room French Renaissance style "home" is the largest private home in the U.S. Built by George Washington Vanderbilt and opened in 1895, it is totally self-sufficient. A tour of the estate is essential. I always try to enjoy lunch in the **Bistro Restaurant**, imbibe a sample or two at the **Winery**, and shop in the stable shops. The **Inn on Biltmore Estate** was recently completed and offers guests a small taste of the Vanderbilts' elegant hospitality and graciousness.

GREENSBORO AREA

I 40 east connects to I 85 which will take you to Greensboro. Here, directly off of I 85, is **Replacements Ltd.** If you have broken your Aunt Frances's tea cup or lost a piece of your wedding silver or dinner service, there is a good chance you will find a replacement piece at this most unique emporium. Even if you don't need anything replaced it is definitely worth a stop.

As you travel I 40 & 85 you will also see signs for wholesale furniture and clothing stores.

OUTER BANKS

A string of islands that begins just over the Virginia state line and extends to Cape Lookout, these barrier islands front the Atlantic Ocean on one side and Pamlico Sound on the other. These islands are particularly beautiful when the summer season is over and the area is not quite so crowded. There is a lot to see: **The Wright Brother's Memorial** at Kitty Hawk, **Cape Hatteras** and **Ocracoke Island**. If traveling in summer, be aware that Saturday is "changeover day," the day rental houses change hands, and the traffic from Norfolk down to the bridge at Kitty Hawk can be awful.

OHIO

Ohio is one of those states that you know is "there," and you know bits and pieces about it, but that's all. It was not until I visited Ohio that I discovered how big a state it is and how beautiful it can be along Lake Erie and the Ohio River.

MARIETTA

Located on the Ohio River, this charming town has a population of about 15,000. **The Lafayette Hotel**, listed on the National Register of Historic Places, is small and very friendly. A short walk from the river, the Lafayette is an official stop of the **Delta Queen**, **American Queen**, and **Mississippi Queen** riverboats. The décor of the hotel includes many antiques, but few more impressive than the eleven-foot pilot wheel from the steamboat *J.D. Ayres* that is featured in the lobby. I thoroughly enjoyed walking Marietta's quiet streets and exploring the antique shops. These shopkeepers were glad to see you whether you bought something or not.

CINCINNATI

A river town, Cincinnati is interesting and upscale. There is a lot to see and do, although my experience has been limited to the downtown area. **The Omni Netherland Plaza Hotel** in downtown Cincinnati is an exceptional example of French Art Deco. The décor, a mix of rosewood, nickel silver, marble, and brass all in a huge public space is magnificent. Two hotel brochures, "An Architectural Walking Tour" and "A Pocket History," will help you find your way around the place. The hotel itself is a part of **Carew Tower**, the "city within a city," full of shops, departments stores, restaurants, and parking. Interestingly, this concept preceded Rockefeller Plaza in New York by four years.

With an unostentatious though very well attended entrance on Vine Street, **The Cincinnatian Hotel** is said to be "The Best in Cincinnati," and you can easily see why. Perfection, graciousness, and elegance on every level is unquestionable. **The Palace Restaurant** is superbly run. The Maitre d' Hotel leaves nothing unattended to—including two beautiful mahogany trays, one with a collection of perfectly displayed reading glasses if you forget yours, and the other with a collection of shawls, in case you feel chilly. This is another one of those elegant destinations that even if you do not spend the night you must see and if possible enjoy a meal or tea. Perhaps the prime reason for the hotel's attention to the needs and wishes of women is that the hotel's General Manager is a woman—as is a fair majority of staff!

Walking around downtown is most enjoyable and there are plenty of art galleries and shops to see. On one trip I found a fabulous treasure—glass flowers that had been illuminated in a bowl. It took me over a week of cleaning and making small repairs but it is a prized find. The city is famous for **Rookwood Pottery**, and **The Rookwood Pottery Restaurant** is a **unique** place to dine.

CLEVELAND

Enjoying something of a renaissance, albeit on sort of a roller coaster, Cleveland has much to offer and its downtown is pleasant. But as with any major city, one should always inquire about safe places to explore. The new ballpark, **Jacobs Field**, has done a lot to contribute to the revival of downtown and restore some civic pride. But if you are going to be in town when the Cleveland Indians are playing, you had best get your tickets ahead of time.

There is a lot to see and do in Cleveland, such as **The Cleveland Museum of Art**, **The Western Reserve Historical Society**, and **The Rock and Roll Hall of Fame**. The former railroad station has been turned into **Terminal Tower**, a shopaholic's delight with a recent 52-story addition. Check out the observation deck for a scenic view of the city.

Within Tower City is **The Ritz–Carlton Cleveland**, accessible by taking an elevator to the main level of the hotel, making for a very secure entrance for women. An excellent way to recoup after shopping is tea at The Ritz, or a visit to **The Century Restaurant** (a la The Twentieth Century Limited). It is a two-part restaurant, the front of which is the more relaxed section with its lighter fare "Orient Express" menu and sushi bar; in back is the more upscale Modern American Cuisine dining room. Adjoining Terminal Tower is **The Renaissance Cleveland Hotel.** It is a beautifully restored facility and the hub of all sorts of activity. I found the staff to be extremely friendly and helpful.

Note: Whenever I have been at Tower City on a Sunday, few restaurants appeared to be open after six (the food court is open until then). The exception is the main dining room at The Renaissance and The Century. If you just want a very light fare in the evening, plan accordingly.

The roads leaving Cleveland when I was there last were a little confusing, and there was a fair amount of construction. Note that the interstate west from Cleveland has two numbers, I 80 and I 90. I 80 comes in from the southeast and I 90 from the north.

During one of my adventures along I 75 through Ohio, I came across **United States Plastic Corp.** in Lima, boasting "The World's Largest Assortments of Plastics." What a find! I bought plastic items in all shapes and sizes and for not very much money.

OKLAHOMA
OKLAHOMA CITY
Oklahoma City seems to me an easy-going, unpretentious place, but it is growing rapidly.

Once when I was being escorted around the city we suddenly came upon a chain link fence covered with notes, tiny stuffed animals, pictures, flowers and many other items, and I completely broke down, for this was the fence in front of where the Federal Building once stood. The tragedy and heartaches were undeniably felt. A new park with its signature memorial chairs is now on the site, and I urge any and all to visit the site. While heart-wrenching, it will help you bring closure (if possible) to one of the tragic events in American History.

Oklahoma City of course offers less sobering diversions, among them **The National Cowboy Hall of Fame** which includes **The Rodeo Hall of Fame, Western Performers Hall of Fame** and the **Hall of Fame Westerners**.

RHODE ISLAND

For such a tiny state, Rhode Island is charming and offers much.

NEWPORT

The drive to Newport from New York City (approx. 185 miles) is easy, provided you avoid summer weekend traffic. Once you cross the Newport Bridge you will quickly discover you are in a different (as in very nice) sort of place. One of the finest "collections" of grand mansions of the Gilded Age can be seen in Newport, opulent, extraordinary, magnificent edifices of the era's industrial barons. Quaintly (and wrongly) referred to as "cottages," they are about as grand as you could possible envision. Many of the "cottages" can be found along **Bellevue Avenue.**

There is so much to see and enjoy in Newport. **Thames Street** is the main street by the water; only in the winter will you find it empty. The small, but elite houses that line the street of this area are maintained to perfection, retaining all of their original beauty and grace. More than any other town in the U.S., Newport boasts over 400 pre-Revolutionary War houses. The oldest Episcopal parish in Rhode Island is **Trinity Church** and **Touro Synagogue** the oldest Synagogue in America. They are within a short walking distance from each other in the older section of Newport. Newport is also home to the **Tennis Hall of Fame** and **Newport Casino**, both worth visiting.

TIVERTON

A short distance from Newport is a quaint, residential, quiet area called Tiverton. It is not pretentious, but seems to be "just right," especially if you like little stores, antique shops and a genuinely friendly ambiance.

From Tiverton drive to Little Compton and Sakonnet. You will not want to rush.

SOUTH CAROLINA

Interstate 95, whether you are heading north or south, will take you right through South Carolina. You know you are getting close to the northern border of South Carolina because you will be amused by the numerous billboards announcing that you are almost at **South of the Border**. This is quite a place for lodging, gas and trinkets, but I'm usually in too much of a hurry to stop.

Yemassee, a tiny (pop. 800), very rural town is just a short distance off of I 95. Friends restored a wonderful old farm in this community and every time I visit I feel like I should be wearing a big hoop skirt. Just off of I 95 by Yemassee there is an outlet store for cutlery and cookware.

Beaufort is a charming place to visit where time has not taken to the fast track. If you saw the movies "The Prince of Tides" or "The Big Chill," then you've been to Beaufort through the magic of the cinema. Antebellum and charismatic, you can tour a few of the homes there. There is also a four-star B & B, **The Rhett House**.

I would not recommend traveling alone late at night on S.C. roads, unless it is a necessity. There are long stretches with virtually nothing, on both the interstate as well as the side roads. There are places where you wouldn't want to get stranded.

SOUTH DAKOTA

Interstate 90 across South Dakota is a great road with some extraordinary sights. At the welcome centers be sure to pick up brochures on various South Dakota places. I found an excellent one, "Guide to Antique Shops in South Dakota."

MITCHELL

Mitchell is about a quarter of the way (heading west) into the state and is definitely a place to stop. And when I was there, the mayor of Mitchell was a woman. While Mitchell contains the usual mix of stores, gas stations and motels, there are a variety of unusual museums: **The Enchanted**

World Doll Museum; The Middle Border Museum of American Indian and Pioneer Life; The International Balloon & Airship Museum, and others.

Then there is the one and only **Corn Palace**. To say it is unique would be an understatement. A huge mosque-like building, the original Corn Palace was built in 1892, moved two blocks away in 1914, and then to the present site in 1921. Aside from the "siding," which features corn sawed lengthwise in half, murals on the walls depict South Dakota lifestyles. The Palace is used for many different events. You can purchase all kinds, and I do mean ALL kinds, of corn products there, a great opportunity to pick up that unusual gift. By the Corn Palace there are antique shops, and there is an antique mall a block or so down the street. There is a doll shop and various tourists' traps as well.

Out of Mitchell the drive along I 90 is a delight, the sights beautiful, and the places to stop many.

BADLANDS NATIONAL PARK
From I 90 heading west you take exit 131 to the northeast entrance to the Badlands. If you are traveling from the west to east then exit at Wall, #110. It has taken 30 million years to produce The Badlands with its multi-colored buttes and rough stone spires. There are three main units in the Badlands. I drove the North Unit, which is a loop road with many scenic overlooks. The interpretive signs along the roadsides are excellent and informative.

WALL
Originally just a place with a drug store, a Catholic Church and less than 500 very poor people, Wall was transformed in 1931 when Dorothy and Ted Hustead bought the drug store, and, after a rough start, started offering water and ice cream to travelers. A burgeoning business was born. Now there are blocks of tourist temptations and **Wall Drug** is now a national institution. Over 20,000 tourists stop at Wall on a typical summer day.

DEADWOOD
Readily accessible from I 90, Deadwood is a real cowboy, stagecoach, and gambling town set in the Black (actually,

dark green) Hills, with 21st century amenities. But a lot of the original flavor of the town has been maintained.

The historic **Franklin Hotel** creaks with history. Its big front porch with rocking chairs allows anyone to sit and watch the world go by. It is too bad that the original and meticulously-laid small tile floor in the main lobby is now practically covered with gambling machines. Granted, it is these machines that bring in the loot to maintain and upgrade the hotel. The wide staircase that is so prominent in the lobby leads to the Emerald Room on the second floor, adjacent to the second floor veranda. It was in the Emerald Room that the ladies of the day would meet. Remember, at the turn of the century, even in the Wild West, the custom was to have separate entrances and places for Ladies and Gentlemen. If by any chance you feel a "spell" coming on, you might want to head for the Emerald Room and the famous Fainting Couch.

The rooms at The Franklin are named after stars that have stayed there. When I was there the recent upgrades and renovations had not yet begun. I had plastic flowers in my suite, as well as a sink in the living room. These accommodations had obviously at one time been an apartment. Nevertheless, I felt secure there, and everything was clean if not quite up-to-date. I did enjoy the real western aura. From all reports (and I did check with the General Manager, Bill Walsh), all has been upgraded and a spa is going in where the Florist Shop and Barber Shop used to be.

1903 is the dining room at The Franklin Hotel and claims to be the oldest dining room in South Dakota. A wonderful pianist plays in 1903 most of the day. The prices are sensible and eating alone is not a problem. I found everyone very friendly.

The town of Deadwood should not be missed. Remember, though, it is a gambling town, with all of the trappings of such places. Some of the signs I saw in a few of the eateries were amusing:

NO SNIVELING
DON'T WORRY YOU'LL NEVER GET OUT OF THIS WORLD ALIVE
NO DANCING ON THE TABLES WITH YOUR SPURS ON

On historic Main Street is the **Midnight Star**, an excellent restaurant that is owned by a South Dakota native and part-time resident by the name of Kevin Costner. (Reservations required.) Although I was alone at a table for two, I had the best time speaking with a couple from Cincinnati at the table adjacent to mine.

There are many attractions to see in Historic Deadwood. The entire city is a designated National Historic Landmark. **Wild Bill Hickok's** and **Calamity Jane's** graves are here, and everyday at the **Old Style Saloon No. 10** Wild Bill's fatal poker game is re-enacted.

Each evening except Sunday deputies pursue and capture Jack McCall on historic Main Street, and all follow to the **Old Town Hall** where the Trial of Jack McCall takes place. A must do! A visit to this historic landmark city is indeed unique.

Just outside of Deadwood heading to Rapid City there is a small strip mall, where I discovered **Maurices**. I had never heard of this apparel store. The people were most friendly, and there on the sale rack I found a well-known designer dress. It had obviously been inventoried for prom season and it was just my size. Reduced to a very nice price, I immediately purchased it and in my mind was already planning to wear it for a Millennium event.

RAPID CITY

About an hour outside Deadwood is Rapid City, where about 20 miles outside the city on a winding road can be found **Mt. Rushmore**. This carved granite tribute to Presidents Washington, Jefferson, Lincoln, and Teddy Roosevelt is definitely something to see. Be sure to go inside the exhibition area and learn just how this massive rock carving was made. It is so huge that a man can stand inside Lincoln's ear. Be prepared, however, for a lot of walking that is not on flat ground.

TENNESSEE
MEMPHIS

Memphis is a happy city that is, from everything that I have experienced there, very friendly for the woman traveler. The two main thoroughfares that I use as compass points are Union and Popular Avenues. It seems that if I can get to either one of them and know which way is downtown, then I can get directly to my destination.

Beale Street, where the Blues were born, opens its arms to the world. Since 1876 **Schwab Dry Goods Store** has been a

Beale Street institution, and its motto tells it all about this emporium: "If you can't find it at Schwab's, you're better off without it." You will get a free, small bag of Schwab goodies just for visiting there. As you walk around the creaky wooden floors, you will probably purchase something you did not expect to want or think you needed, much less think you would find. Up the stairs is "the museum," relics of old Schwab's and Memphis. Every time I've been on Beale Street I've been entertained by a group of young Memphis boys who perform unbelievable gymnastic feats on the street. No padding, no nets—they are truly amazing. Music fills Beale Street. The clubs line each side of the street and what is not a club is probably a tourist shop or music store or history shop of sorts. In case you are looking for voodoo potions, they can be found in Schwab's and probably other shops as well. And do not leave Beale Street or Memphis without having Elvis's favorite: a fried peanut butter and banana sandwich.

Within walking distance of Beale Street is the historic **Peabody Hotel**, where the famous Peabody ducks live in their duck penthouse, when they are not swimming and preening in the lobby fountain. The penthouse can be visited by the public and is a must-see. Then there is the Duck March: a few minutes before 11 a.m. each day a red carpet is rolled out from the elevator to the lobby's massive marble fountain. At exactly 11 a.m., escorted by the Duck Master and with a John Phillip Sousa March playing, the ducks parade and "walk" on the red carpet and into the fountain where they enjoy the day. At 5 p.m. the procedure is reversed and they return to their penthouse for the night. It is hard to frown at The Peabody.

To paraphrase what historian David Cohn has said: "The Mississippi Delta begins in the lobby of The Peabody . . . and ultimately you will see everybody who is anybody in the Delta." Indeed, the bar in the lobby of The Peabody is truly congenial. Sitting silently alone at the bar does not last long, as conversations start quickly. Of course, if you decide to be stone faced and aloof, then people will ignore you. Music always fills the air in the Peabody lobby. The informal **Dux** and **Mallards** restaurants are comfortable and at **Café Expresso** you can indulge in homemade ice cream or a Peabody signature Vanilla muffin. If possible enjoy the best of ultimate dining at the exquisite **Chez Phillip**. The Peabody also has one of the best memorabilia rooms of any hotel. You step back in time, with a taped narration that begins with the music "Thanks for the Memories" and continues with the history of The Peabody.

With the Peabody as your hub, you will be able to walk and sightsee much of the area. You will find an eclectic mix of shops, including a wonderful fully stocked mini grocery store, **The Market on Main Street**, that includes a first-rate deli department. As for museums, Memphis has **The Peabody Place Museum**, with its exceptional Chinese exhibit. A short distance from the Peabody is **The Dixon Gallery**, a small charming art gallery that adjoins the former Dixon residence. You can't be in Memphis and not go to **Graceland**, Elvis Presley's home. I didn't know what to expect at Graceland, but it turned out to be fascinating seeing the King's home as well as the collection of elaborate costumes, cars, motorcycles, and his airplane with its large bed. I talked about it for weeks. **Sun Recording Studios** is a small gem of a place, where many careers have been launched. Be sure to take the tour.

A couple of shopping notables are **The Women's Exchange**, where handmade items are exquisite and the luncheon fare absolutely Southern delicious. **The Belz Outlet** is just outside of Memphis on I 40.

NASHVILLE
Country music is in the air in Nashville, even if in reality it is only imaginary. Nashville is a savvy town where not all of the women wear Minnie Pearl hats and not all of the men carry guitars.

The **Grand Old Opry** is a must-see and you will definitely not feel alone. Before you get seated and comfortable you will be talking with the people around you. **The Hermitage Hotel** is a treasure of a place that is currently undergoing restoration. You can walk to the corner and get a Nashville Sightseeing Trolley, which (as of this writing) costs about $3.00 for an all day pass. There are several different tours, but you can simply get off the trolley if you want to stroll for a while and pick up the next trolley. You can also take a self-guided walking tour right from the hotel. You get your map and follow the markings *on the sidewalk* outside the hotel. I wish more cities had this.

The **Union Station Hotel** should not be missed. The restoration of this magnificent train station is impressive. It is accessible from the trolley.

GREENEVILLE

If you take US 11 east off of I 81 for about 10 miles you will come across a town that looks as though it leapt out of a Grandma Moses painting. Historic Greeneville is "The Place To Be," boasts the Historic Greeneville Shopping and Visitors Guide, and I wholeheartedly agree. Clean and charming, upscale in a countrified way, I have not found anything or anyone to dislike about Greeneville. Its modest population of 13,500 souls are fairly well spread out, so there is never a feeling of "crowd" in this charming place.

The historic district is a twelve-block area, which you could see easily in a day. There are antique stores and shops plus a mini shopping center with grocery store and drug store. Curiously, there seems to be an abundance of lawyers' shingles along the streets as well. I have yet to figure that one out. Lunch at **Tipton's Café** on West Depot Street is a must! It is small—no, tiny—but wonderful, and you will be treated like a native.

The charming hotel on north Main Street, **General Morgan Inn**, is indeed special. Unpretentious but delightful with subtle upscale amenities, this charming hotel in "downtown" has comfortable dining rooms with superb food served in a friendly and prompt manner. Of the three dining areas, my favorite is **The Library**. **The Blue Bar** is cozy and just fine for sitting by yourself. The bedrooms are very comfortable, and the views from the windows picturesque; from the window in my room, I could see at least six church steeples.

TEXAS

Being such a big state, Texas has long stretches of highway with few services. Be sure to top off the gas tank (and your stomach) whenever you can. I've done the drive from Santa Fe, New Mexico to Dallas in a day, and it's a long haul. In Amarillo you pick up US 287 (from I 40), a good road that takes you through some delightful and interesting towns. **Clarendon** (pop. 2,067) offered **1929 Landmark Subs & Sodas**, **Coyote Den Books**, and the **It'll**

Do Motel. Hedley (pop 391) had tempting fruit stands. Big signs for peaches. Memphis (pop 2,465) has antique shops and a Tea Room. Childress (pop 6,664) is the area's point for shipping and supplies for the neighboring grain and cattle ranches. Proudly displayed as you drive through town: HOMETOWN OF ROY COOPER, 8 times World Champion Calf Roper. Other sights: Restwell Motel as well as the usual chain motels, a sign stating All Handmade Quilts in front of a small house, a Dollar General Store, Pizza Hut, Morgan's Catfish Diner (At least I think that was the name) and a sign for The Heritage Museum. In its heyday, this must have been quite a town. In Iowa Park I came across what I thought was a cattle ranch, then my bleary eyes (it was 7 p.m.) focussed on the "livestock": camels.

DALLAS

Dallas is flat and spread out, an ever-expanding city whose downtown is enjoying a revival after undergoing a bit of a slump. I like Dallas a lot, though it takes some getting used to . . . but that is true about a lot of places. Driving might be a bit of a challenge for the visitor. I definitely recommend parking your car and taking public transportation.

The historic Adolphus Hotel is magnificent and located in the center of downtown. Everything about The Adolphus is outstanding, and the artwork is impressive. Tea in the afternoon at The Adolphus is a tradition that gives one a special feeling of old world charm. Piano music permeates the air as you sip your tea and relax in the exquisite surroundings. At The Adolphus there is an informal dining room, The Bistro, cozy and friendly, and then the ultimate dining pleasure, The French Room. For many, the French Room is a standing tradition for special events. I have eaten alone there and suddenly realized other women were doing likewise.

Two blocks from The Adolphus is the original Neiman Marcus, and there is not a thing within these walls that you wouldn't want. You can have lunch in The Zodiac Restaurant, where their signature popovers will delight you and energize you.

The Melrose Hotel is a charming boutique hotel slightly out of the downtown area. Lovely moldings, thick walls, and glass door knobs all recall an earlier era. Parking is conveniently on-site, and the hotel has a complementary car service to downtown. **The Library Bar** is an "in" meeting place and has been voted the best piano and martini bar in Dallas. **The Landmark Restaurant** has also won awards and is comfortable for all. From the interstate The Melrose is easy to find with directions provided by the hotel staff.

The Mansion on Turtle Creek is a stately hotel that was originally a private home. It has since added a 142-room hotel tower. Today one dines in what was the original living room of the mansion; the current bar was the original dining room. The bar truly evokes the era of the oil barons. The rooms are nicely appointed and spacious with some having a small garden and appropriately called garden rooms.

There is a lot to see and enjoy in Dallas, so be sure to check the newspapers and with the hotel concierge. There is a museum dedicated to the Kennedy Assassination in Dallas in 1963. It is located in the building in which Lee Harvey Oswald fired the fatal shots, The Texas School Book Depository.

UTAH

Coming into Utah on I 80 from the east the landscape changes dramatically, from high plains to huge red rock formations. The traffic changes dramatically, too, as you approach Salt Lake City. The roads seem to always be under construction, a condition that will probably last until Salt Lake City hosts the Winter Olympics in 2002.

SUNDANCE

Approximately twenty minutes from Provo and perhaps an hour from Salt Lake City, Sundance is an easy and beautiful drive, at least in the summer. It is the home of Robert Redford's Sundance Resort and Institute, a community for art and nature. The various accommodations are handsome (especially if you like the log-cabin look), clean and safe. When one checks in, one's key is attached to a small flashlight; accommodations are snuggled in the woods and it can be a very dark walk from your car to the front door.

The shops are tempting and the restaurants are excellent.

Because in Utah you must belong to a "Club" to have a drink, at Sundance (as at other places), you become a member of the Sundance "Club" when you check in.

The spectacular national parks of Utah (Bryce Canyon, Zion, Arches, Canyonlands) are within a day's driving distance of Sundance and really should be seen. Amfac Parks and Resorts Company (303-297-5757) handles accommodations at Bryce and Zion, while the little town of Moab is the place to stay for a visit to Arches and Canyonlands.

VIRGINIA

Virginia is a state full of history and beauty. The highways are excellent and the scenic drives are magnificent, particularly in the fall. Roads are well marked. The scenic highways, specifically the Blue Ridge Parkway and the Skyline Drive, can be break burners in places.

I consider Virginia a gentle and civilized state, but of course I live there. Although my mother was born in Virginia, my parents met in Virginia and are now buried there, I was raised in New York City, so as a little girl visiting Virginia relatives they would call me a Yankee.

The Atlantic Ocean, Chesapeake Bay and the James, Elizabeth, Rappahannock, and Potomac Rivers all create beautiful river edges and coastlines. The beaches are clean, the ocean spectacular.

RICHMOND

History abounds in this attractive, diversified city. There is a mix of architecture—Greek revival, Victorian, antebellum, federal, "just southern," and modern. As a commercial center, Richmond is home to many Fortune 500 companies. As for accommodations, **The Jefferson Hotel** is grand and stately. If you can't stay there, the next best thing would be to enjoy grand dining at five-diamond **Lemaire Restaurant**, or more casual fare at **T.J.'s.**

There is also an elegant afternoon tea. If nothing else, obtain a brochure at the front desk and be sure to tour this outstanding property and visit the hotel's museum right off the main lobby. To think that this hotel was almost demolished is frightening.

A few blocks from the Jefferson, but possibly a little too far to walk, is a favorite of mine for very informal, friendly dining—it is **Perly's Restaurant.** Try their Brunswick Stew or hot dog with "the works." And save room for dessert.

Hollywood Cemetery, a five-minute drive from the Jefferson, is one of the most beautiful cemeteries in the country and well worth a drive around. Presidents James Monroe and John Tyler are buried there, as well as Confederate President Jefferson Davis. Be sure to see The Confederate Soldiers Section, where approximately 18,000 soldiers are buried, as well as the impressive Pyramid. **Shockoe Bottom**, now a thriving residential area with a farmers market, art enter, eclectic mix of restaurants, and an exciting live-music scene is something for all to enjoy. **The Fan District** is a unique area of Richmond near Virginia Commonwealth University. Within it is St. John's Church, where Patrick Henry delivered his famous speech in 1775.

A walk along the James River is a delightful way to spend an afternoon. Other "don't misses" are **Monument Avenue**, the **Virginia Science Museum**, which was originally Broad Street Train Station, the **Virginia Museum of Fine Arts** and the **Valentine Richmond History Center**.

NORFOLK

Originally known primarily as a huge Navy base, Norfolk is growing and becoming a highly diversified city. The artistic jewel in Norfolk's crown is **The Chrysler Museum**. A spectacular, small, world-class museum, this treasure should not be overlooked. Their restaurant, **Phantoms**, is a cozy spot to dine, and the prices are reasonable. The Chrysler Museum also operates two historic houses a short distance from downtown, **Moses Myers House** (1792) and the **Willoughby-Baylor House**. **Waterside**, a collection of stores and restaurants on the Elizabeth River, is an eclectic mix of shopping and eating. One can take a ferry from Waterside over to Portsmouth and walk around Old Towne Portsmouth, visit the outstanding Children's Museum and other attractions, and take the ferry back. You can also take (in season) the **Carrie B** sightseeing boat for a tour of the Elizabeth River. More extended water tours and dining are available on the **Spirit of Norfolk**. Reservations are required. The National Maritime Center, **Nauticus**, with the added attraction of the **Battleship Wisconsin** berthed alongside, is a new major downtown attraction. At **The MacArthur Memorial**, also in downtown, admission is free, and here one can view General MacArthur's five thousand books, two million items of correspondence, and a 24-minute film on the life of the controversial General. (You should see the movie first, however.) Also, the new **MacArthur Mall** in downtown is state-of-the-art (as malls go) and teams with wonderful stores and a well-run food court. The ever-expanding **Norfolk Zoo** is attractive and most pleasant for a change of pace.

On west 22nd Street in Norfolk is **Rowena's**, where you can recharge your batteries in the Tea Room or just sample some of Rowena's gourmet delights.

A very wonderful restaurant with some of the best choices and presentations of foods is **The Bistro** in downtown. A fine restaurant with eclectic décor and ambiance is **Bobbywood** on Granby Street. And then there is **The Painted Lady** on 17th Street, a combination restaurant and boutique, where live music is performed on Fridays and Saturdays.

Note: When leaving the Norfolk area check your map carefully. If you are going north on I 64, there are two ways to approach the interstate: the Hampton Roads Bridge Tunnel, or via The Monitor Merrimack Bridge. If traveling in rush hour, the latter is the way to go. A few miles longer, there are rarely any delays. Huge delays often occur on the Hampton Roads Bridge Tunnel—and there is no turning around.

VIRGINIA BEACH
Virginia Beach has a little bit of everything. The beachfront area in the summer affords a full array of beach life. There is a new concrete "boardwalk" as well as a bicycle trail. **The Marine Science Museum** is outstanding. Some historic sights include **The Old Coast Guard Station**, the oldest government built lighthouse at **Cape Henry**, and the **First Landing Cross**, marking where the first settlers arrived in 1607.

THE CHESAPEAKE BAY BRIDGE TUNNEL
This impressive engineering feat spans the Chesapeake Bay from Virginia Beach to the Eastern Shore of Virginia—19 miles. The toll is $10.00 each way. The time you save going north (95 miles and 1½ hours for the trek to New York) and the pleasure of traveling up the Eastern Shore allows one to forget the cost. When the Bridge-Tunnel opened, it also opened the Eastern Shore to the mainland. Prior to its opening access to the main-

land was by ferryboat only, or by traveling up to Maryland and across the Chesapeake Bridge to Annapolis.

THE EASTERN SHORE

The Eastern Shore of Virginia is really beginning to be discovered. A peninsula with the Atlantic Ocean on one side and The Chesapeake Bay on the other, it is (for now) truly a beautiful rural area. Farming has been the main industry, potatoes and soybeans being the principle crops. For years it was isolated, but when the Chesapeake Bay Bridge Tunnel was built, life on the Eastern Shore changed forever.

Arriving on the Eastern Shore via the Bridge-Tunnel you are on Route 13, which will take you north. **ShoreBreak** Restaurant with its good food and pleasant atmosphere is 9 miles north of the Bridge-Tunnel on Route 13. (If you mention this book, you may just get a freebee.) Approximately a mile north from ShoreBreak on Route 13 and to the left is **Cape Charles**, a small historic town with a beautiful waterfront on the Chesapeake, where many of the large old homes are becoming bed and breakfast establishments. **Charmar's Antiques and Collectibles** on Mason Street is a great place to shop. If you have your golf clubs with you, you can enjoy the new **Bay Creek Golf Course** in Cape Charles that carries Arnold Palmer's signature.

Heading north on 13 you pass such towns as **Eastville**, and **Nassawadox**, where the hospital is located. In **Melfa**, going north, make a left and look for the **Blue Crab Bay Co.**, where you can find the best "shore-themed" products. You might want to schedule a stop in **Chincoteague** to take in the National Wildlife Refuge and famous wild ponies (Remember Misty?). This beautiful place has definitely become a bit touristy, so off-season is ideal.

Don't leave the Eastern Shore without having a *real* Eastern Shore crab cake. You will also find fresh produce stands and seafood for sale along Route 13. Also there are lots of antique shops to "pick at."

HAMPTON

Worth seeing here is the **Virginia Air and Space Center**, the official visitor center of NASA Langley Research Center. The exhibits are interesting and well presented. There is an IMAX theater as well.

NEWPORT NEWS

One of the most charming museums is the **Mariners Museum**, which is a short drive off of I 64. Call the museum for specific directions. It is easy to find and well worth the visit.

WILLIAMSBURG, JAMESTOWN, YORKTOWN

This is the area where it all began. Historic **Williamsburg** is a treasure, but requires a sturdy pair of walking shoes. You will not only walk a lot, but many of the streets are cobblestone, not great for feet. To visit inside the historic areas tickets must be purchased at the visitor's center. Tickets are a little pricey, but to maintain and preserve this treasure admission fees are a necessity. The **College of William and Mary** is in the center of town and a small college gem. About a 5-10 minute drive from the heart of Williamsburg is the famous **Williamsburg Pottery**. Originally known for its real bargains, "the pottery" has grown to include all sorts of things at all sorts of prices. And at 200 acres, this is not a place you can simply spend five minutes at. Again, walking shoes and sensible clothing (especially during summer) are advised. Outlet stores of every variety can be found on Richmond Road, but keep in mind that "outlet" does not always mean "bargain."

A couple of theme parks, **Busch Gardens** and **Water-Country USA**, are also nearby.

While in the area a detour of sorts on Rt. 17 is highly recommended. Here you will find lots of antique shops and thrift shops of all varieties. You will cross the Coleman Bridge where the toll is $2.00, but you pay it only once on the northbound side. In **Irvington** you will find **The Hope and Glory Inn**. Originally a school in the 1890s, the building has been renovated into one of the "101 Best Hotels in the World," according to the *Tatler/Cunard Travel Guide*. Rates are not exorbitant; rooms begin around $130 and Cottages $155 and include a homemade breakfast. **The Trick Dog Café** has recently opened for dinner Tuesday–Saturday and for brunch on Sunday. The décor is subtly sophisticated and the "right" music fills the air. The menu is exceptional and the prices not exorbitant. The bar is female inviting in just the right way, so being alone is not a problem. Don't you love a bar menu that simply states on one side: SIT and STAY?

The town of Irvington consists of but a city few blocks, but there are several nice shops to entice you. **The Dandelion** (apparel and gifts) has just what you have secretly wanted to add to your wardrobe. Stopping at the kitchen shop, **Time to Cook**, nearly got me back in the kitchen again in a serious way. **Duncan & Drake**, an eclectically filled shop of colorful merchandise, opposite the Hope and Glory Inn

The famous **Tides Inn**, under its new owners, is undergoing major renovation. What it will become is yet to be known but with its location and history, it is hard to be believe that it won't be special.

Between Williamsburg and Richmond along Route 5 are the **James River Plantations**, where you can visit manor homes filled with antiques, beauty and history. Fine dining establishments and charming bed and breakfast accommodations are also available along this beautiful route. Many places overlook the James River.

CHARLOTTESVILLE

A lovely town with history, style and (according to *U.S. News and World Report*) the second best public university in the country, Charlottesville merits a few days of your time. Save the better part of a day to tour **Monticello**, the home of Mr. Thomas Jefferson. Jefferson's other creation, **The University of Virginia**, is an "academic village" with broad lawns, serpentine brick walls, and magnificent rotunda.

ORANGE

About 35 minutes from Charlottesville is Orange, sight of Dolley and James Madison's home, **Montpelier**. The well-known **Willow Grove Inn**, where the food is superb, offers accommodations in one of their perfectly appointed rooms or cottages. Also in Orange is the campus of **Woodberry Forest**, a prestigious boys' school. The grounds and buildings are definitely worth a drive around.

Going north on I 64 from Charlottesville, **Waynesboro** will be your first big town. This is where you get on The Blue Ridge Parkway but before doing so be sure to top off the tank.

STAUNTON

Staunton (pronounced STAN-ton) is an enjoyable place that has become too big to be called quaint. Museums, a historic area, and lots of antique shops all make this place appealing. **The Woodrow Wilson Birthplace and Museum** is on North Coalter Street and is easy to find. Two other places to visit are the **Museum of American Frontier Culture**, and the **Statler Brothers Complex** about a mile from downtown.

HOT SPRINGS

The drive to Hot Springs is not difficult, except perhaps in winter when there may be snow and ice on the roads. In Hot Springs is the magnificent 15,000-acre **The Homestead**, a one-of-a-kind resort where you can golf, horseback ride, fish, hike, ski, ice-skate, and more. Dining at The Homestead is a first rate, culinary delight with several options. **The Main Dining Room** is large and magnificent with an inviting dance floor. **The Grill** is cozy and exceptional, and **The Commonwealth Room** more informal, but not any less stylish.

A few miles up the road are the original warm springs baths, to which the hotel provides complementary transportation. Bathing can be done au natural if you like, since "taking the waters" is supposed to be absolutely beneficial to one both inside and out. The water temperature is about 98 degrees and there is a large variety of minerals in the springs. There are two spring facilities, one for the ladies and one for the men. I have been in these springs when the temperature was in the low teens outside. Incidentally, if it is in the low teens outside, it is almost the same inside the bathhouse. Under these conditions you waste no time getting into the warm springs. The real challenge comes when you get out of the warm springs and into your clothes. If you indulge in the winter, forget fashion; just take extra warm clothes, socks, boots, gloves and a hat to put on when you get out. It is truly an experience not to be missed.

Speaking of healthy pursuits, The Spa at The Homestead is exceptional. Give yourself a treat from head to toe. A swim in the huge indoor pool, which is fed from the heated mineral springs, always helps me to make room for the next scrumptious meal. Walking the hills also helps. There are sports of every variety for every season, and then there are the inside activities, which can range from wine tasting to a cooking class to a fashion show to dancing lessons. The challenge at The Homestead is not finding something to do, but fitting it all in during your stay.

There are lots of tempting shops at The Homestead. The tiny village of Hot Springs is charming and the area homes are attractive. Check with the hotel as for special events, such as women's weekends.

ABINGDON

This enchanting quaint town in the highlands of Virginia is just over the border from Tennessee. It is easily accessible from I 81 and many other highways. Abingdon is the home of the historic Barter Theater and the award-winning **Camberley's Martha Washington Inn.** A stay at the Inn is a delight and the service you will receive will be memorable. Main Street is a treasure trove of clothing and antique shops. Obtain a brochure and "do" the self-guided walking tour of Abingdon's Downtown Historic District. Five minutes from the Inn is **Dixie Pottery**. It is full of wonderfully useful items, all sensibly discounted, as well as items you probably hadn't thought about. For cinema buffs, **The Famous Moonlight Drive In Movie Theater** is a stone's throw away from Dixie Pottery.

WASHINGTON, D.C.

The roadways into D.C. are confusing and difficult. Be sure to study a map. It will help—a little. Don't listen to the natives who say driving around and in our nation's Capital is easy. Trust me, it isn't. Know exactly where you are going. Obtain directions from a competent informant. "Rehearse" in your mind how you are going to get where you want to go and know the exits by heart, because you can't stop and check very easily where you are or what you just passed. I suggest that you park your car in a reputable garage near a suburban metro station and take the metro. When in Washington, plan to walk or take taxis. You may spend a few extra pennies but the time you save will make it all worthwhile.

A historic gem of a hotel on Pennsylvania Avenue, **The Willard** is where the last negotiations of the Civil War were held. (The Northerners would only walk in the north door and the Southerners in the south door.) For formal dining there is the **Willard Room**, and for informal fare there is **Café 1401**. A drink in the **Round Robin Bar**, a Washington landmark, should not be missed even if you just sit, watch and enjoy a Shirley Temple.

There are many sights and shops to visit near The Willard. **The Occidental** is next to the Willard and a historic property as well. **The Pavilion at the Old Post Office** has plenty of shops and eateries of all varieties. The oldest saloon in Washington (founded in 1859), **Ebbitt's Grill** is within walking distance from The Willard. This is a very popular rendezvous spot so call for a reservation. I also like the **M & S Grill**, just down the street.

WEST VIRGINIA

Hopefully you will have a reason to go to White Sulphur Springs, West Virginia and see **The Greenbrier**. An exit off of I 64, White Sulphur Springs is almost a ghost town now, although it has a few modern stores. Its original charm can still be found in several antique shops and **Bev's Diner**, where I enjoyed a delicious BLT, fresh homemade pie, and coffee.

What anchors White Sulphur Springs is **The Greenbrier Hotel Resort.** It is hard to describe adequately, although I will give it a cursory try. Unique, huge, with immense bright color prints as background for exquisite antiques. Bright white glossy woodwork and trim frames each room. It is easy to get lost as you wonder the hallways, but what splendor in which to get lost! The top-secret Government Relocation Facility, designed to accommodate the U.S. Senate and House of Representatives in the event of a nuclear war, was clandestinely built (between 1958–1961) under part of the hotel. It was totally maintained in complete readiness for 30 years until 1992 when the Washington Post revealed its whereabouts. Dismantling of the facility began immediately and was completed in 1995. The lease between the Government and The Greenbrier was thereupon terminated. Today, tours are available of this fascinating facility. Reservations are required.

The shops at The Greenbrier will not disappoint you. Aside from the grand hotel, resort and spa, there is also **The Greenbrier Clinic**. It is an absolute state of the art clinic, where one can go and get a complete physical. Three times a week trains come to White Sulphur from Washington.

Leaving White Sulphur Springs just past Beckley is **Tamarack**, a statewide collection of handmade crafts, art and cuisine to tempt the traveler. This is a place where one should stop and shop and take home some of the best of West Virginia Crafts. There is a Food Court that is serviced by The Greenbrier, and also The Greenbrier Shop where you can buy all sorts of gourmet coffees and delectables.

PARKERSBURG

It is not difficult to see that the river city of Parkersburg once saw grander days, although there still is a lot going on and probably before too long will experience a rebirth. Interstate 77S, to exit 176 to 50 W, took me to **The Historic Blennerhassett Hotel**. Greeted by a most pleasant young bellman/doorman who took my bag and parked my car, I found myself in an unpretentious hotel with charm and obvious history. It was only an overnight stay, but what looms in my memory is the genuine friendliness, cleanliness and quiet comfort. Also, the long rectangular dining room was where I experienced an excellent cuisine with exceptional service. The maitre d' as well as overseer of the bar was a Tom Selleck look-alike, who was professional and checked on every guest. He fixed me a spiced warm shrimp appetizer, homemade rolls and a light drink for my dinner.

WISCONSIN
KOHLER

Two and a half hours from Chicago and an hour from Milwaukee, Kohler, Wisconsin might be considered a sort of fiefdom, since it is the "company town" of the well-known manufacturer of plumbing fixtures and supplies. It is a very manicured town, extremely clean, pristine and safe. **The American Club**, originally established as lodging facilities for the craftsmen Mr. Kohler had brought in to work at his factory, is now restored and refurbished and open to the public. This charming, beautiful, resort hotel (AAA Five Diamond!) quite naturally contains state-of-the-art bath fixtures, alone worth a night's tariff. A tour of the Kohler plant is fascinating as is the Kohler Design Center. After spending but a few minutes inside, you will want to change all the plumbing in your home.

DODGEVILLE

Dodgeville, approximately 130 miles from Milwaukee, is home to **The House on the Rock**, an unbelievable place that is impossible to describe in a paragraph. If you are a pack rat you will feel right at home and your collections will look puny by miles. To see what Alex Jordan envisioned and accomplished is mind-boggling. There is the glass walled Infinity Room, with no visible supports, that projects 218 feet out into the Wyoming Valley; the Tiffany inspired lamp collection; the antique weapons room; the collections of toys, banks, glass, dolls, doll houses, musical instruments, miniatures of all varieties; the huge pipe organ that seems to envelope you; and the purported largest carousel in the world—and this describes only a part of this most unique site. Call for details. Admission prices vary according to season and age, approx. $4.00-$16.00

SPRING GREEN

Approximately five miles on Route 14 from The House on The Rock is Spring Green, and Frank Lloyd Wright's **Taliesin**. Here you will learn and get to know the master architect. There are several tours available. Some require reservations. Walking shoes are a must. There is a café on site. Call for information.

WYOMING
WAMSUTTER

Every traveler needs one of these stories. In this town (Pop. 240) I received a warning citation from the Police Chief himself. The citation reads: Stop sign violation at Kelly & McCormick. I had a friend with me. She and I were thirsty and I decided to turn off of I 80. We had left Cheyenne and Laramie and were heading west to Salt Lake. Seeing a sign for a cafe we turned off of I 80 and found ourselves on a very, very dusty road. The wind was blowing dust everywhere. We decided that maybe we weren't as thirsty as we had thought. Suddenly a shiny police car with very bright flashing lights and a noisy siren came up behind me. "What had I done?" I asked my friend. "I don't know" she replied. The Chief of Police had me get out of the car. He was very nice and it turned out that I had neglected to stop at the stop sign. We talked. He told me about his family and the dirt bike that his children had. I told him about my project and that "sir I did not see any stop sign, with the dust blowing." After more conversation, he smiled and handed me what he said was " decoration for my refrigerator door." For that I will always remember Wamsutter.

CASPER AND CHEYENNE

Casper and Cheyenne are the two largest "cities" in Wyoming, each with a population of about 45,000. They are some 150 miles apart, however, so plan accordingly if making the trek across Wyoming. There are few other towns in the state with city-like amenities. Casper has a **Hampton Inn**, among other hotels, which I am pleased to note is managed by a woman. The roads away from Casper and Cheyenne are strikingly beautiful, especially toward the west, but services are few and far between. Even towns that may be prominently marked on the map can be little more than intersections.

JACKSON HOLE

Years ago my older son had gone to camp in this area and subsequently had become a counselor. He always raved about how spectacular the scenery was, how fantastic rafting on the Snake was, hiking and the wonderful horseback riding. I didn't doubt it, but only when I saw it years later did I realize how true were his words and observations.

Jackson is upscale, well heeled, tony and the scenery magnificent. Everyone is "good-lookingly healthy." The Grand Tetons are totally and absolutely awesome. Jackson Hole in the summer is filled with tourists, but it is not objectionable—except perhaps to the natives. The private homes are impressive and the scenery only adds to this unbelievable setting.

You will find everything you might need in town from the very upscale to the touristy trinket. From some young Jacksonites I learned of some second hand shops/thrift shops. I found some items and in fact an engraved silver-plated plate from my sons' school in Virginia! Small world indeed. It was fun to explore these shops in such a different area.

There are many places to stay in Jackson. I have stayed twice at **The Parkway Inn**. Very convenient to town. The parking is easy on site. The décor in the rooms is pleasing with attractive antiques and handmade quilts on the beds. There is a delicious complementary breakfast served in the breakfast lounge. It is here where everyone seems to meet and discuss his or her Wyoming agendas.

YELLOWSTONE NATIONAL PARK:
I drove from Jackson and entered the park at the south entrance. I was going to drive the Grand Loop, which you will understand when you look at the map. My first real stop was at Old Faithful and The Old Faithful Inn. Be sure to go inside this most unique structure. I spent the first night at the Lake Yellowstone Hotel. Delightful. What scenery! The next day I drove and was still in awe of the scenery and spent the night at Mammoth Hot Springs. So much beauty!

God Bless America. It's the best!